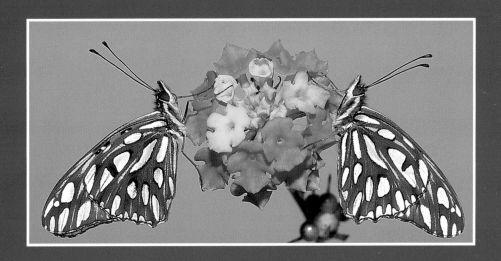

The little caterpillar creeps
Awhile before in silk it sleeps.
It sleeps awhile before it flies,
And flies awhile before it dies,
And that's the end of three good tries.

David McCord

Whites & Sulphurs

Family: Pieridae

These are among the most common butterflies, both in Florida and worldwide. They are also among the most migratory butterfly species. The name Pieridae comes from Piera, a district in the ancient land of Thessaly in northern Greece and home of the nine Muses, goddesses who presided over poetry and song.

The flight style of Pierids consists of almost constant wing flapping rather than a combination of flapping and soaring. Pierids usually prefer bright, sunny places.

Pierids have a unique way of raising their body temperature. While basking in the sun, they hold their wings at an angle which reflects light toward their dark bodies.

Great Southern White

△ The Great Southern White is known for its distinctive, blue-tipped antennae.

This butterfly breeds year round on islands along the East Coast of Florida. However, it does not usually breed at the same place every time. It moves up and down the coast in search of food, sometimes in large numbers. When it encounters strong winds, it may fly low along the leeward side of coastal sand dunes to avoid being blown off course.

The Great Southern White is a common butterfly across southern Florida and throughout the Keys. Males are white and have an irregular black border along the outer margin and tip of the forewing, while the males of the Florida White are almost pure white. Females are more heavily marked with black, have a dark spot in the center of the forewing, and the rest of the wing varies from white to dark grey in color. The adults are usually found flying over salt marshes along the coast, and occasionally reproduce in great numbers, with some of the overflow population moving northward along the coastline. The adults lay their yellowish eggs on leaves of saltwort. The yellow larvae have grey stripes and small black bumps; the black-and-white pupa mimics a bird dropping.

Ascia monuste phileta. Range in Florida: Southern half of the mainland and the Florida Keys, occasionally further north. Maximum wingspan 2-2.3 inches. Months seen: all year. Caterpillar food: saltwort, pepper-grass, and capers.

BUTTERFLIES ARE TOUGH

In the wrenching climax to "All's Quiet on the Western Front," a young soldier is fatally distracted by a butterfly which flits across a scene of battlefield devastation, a symbol of the beauty and fragility of nature in the midst of human violence. Such bold behaviour is absolutely typical of butterflies, which are not particularly fragile but tough, wary, and resilient. They are at home in harsh environments, from the arctic tundra and high mountains to deserts and the canyons between skyscrapers.

In Florida, butterflies suddenly materialize in the steamy aftermath of violent thunderstorms. They sip on the nectar of roadside patches of Spanish needles along I-75, unperturbed by the rush of six lanes of heavy traffic. They can be seen in the smaller Florida Keys, beating their way upwind in a stiff breeze that is ready to sweep them off in the general direction of Colombia if they miss their perch.

A butterfly may seem to dance frivolously from flower to flower in the garden, but yesterday it may have flapped across Lake Okeechobee, with hungry bass waiting for it to falter in a down-draft.

MD

A GOOD REASON TO LEARN ABOUT BUTTERFLIES

The knowing eye always sees more. Awareness is remarkably dependent upon knowledge, so that being able to recognize a buckeye, or a blue, seems to increase the number of these species in the most miraculous manner. The naturalist lives in a world that is far more pleasing than that of the non-naturalist. This phenomenon has no known limits. Nature provides an endless parade of rare events, so that for the more knowledgeable butterfly watcher, spotting a Pipevine Swallowtail in Miami or a Polydamus Swallowtail in Gainseville is enough to imbue a whole morning with a sense of specialness, a background aura of fortunate surprise.

MD

Cabbage White

The European Cabbage Butterfly, or Cabbage White, was accidentally introduced into Quebec, Canada, around 1860, probably as larvae on imported cabbages. From that point, it spread quickly across most of North America. The genus name, *Pieris*, is derived from the name of a goddess in Greek mythology, and the species name, *rapae*, comes from the Latin word for turnip. In Florida, this butterfly is rare south of Orlando, seemingly unable to take the hot summers. In north Florida it is seen throughout the year, but it is more common in springtime.

In cabbage or mustard fields, male Cabbage Whites may be seen courting females by hovering over them. Usually, because the female has already mated soon after emerging from her pupa, she will reject any new courting males by spreading her wings out flat and raising her abdomen into the air, making mating almost impossible.

The adult butterflies feed on an extremely wide range of flowering plants. The caterpillars are agricultural pests on a variety of green vegetables, but they also feed on wild plants.

The Cabbage White butterfly employs an unusual device to give its young an advantage. When the female lays her eggs,

she also marks the plant on which the eggs are laid with a chemical perfume which tends to repel other butterflies, thus giving her offspring a monopoly on the tasty leaves of that particular plant.

Pieris rapae. Range in Florida: mostly north of Orlando. Maximum wingspread: 1.5 - 2 inches. Months seen: every month. Caterpillar food: crucifers such as cabbage, collards, broccoli, and mustards.

THE HARMLESS BUTTERFLY

Butterflies do not bite or carry disease. In their adult form, they do no harm. And, unlike most other insects, they have very colorful and beautiful wings. Their spectacular colors and patterns can only be equalled in nature by those of birds.

Family: Pieridae

Florida White

The population of Florida Whites rises and falls dramatically. In some years, this species may be quite common in the shade of south Florida's tropical hammocks, less common in other years. The males have a fast, erratic flight and fly through the tops of trees. Females are easier to observe because they are usually found fluttering more slowly at lower levels within the hammocks, looking for food plants. Adults are sometimes caught in the webs of golden silk spiders. Occasionally, Florida Whites wander northward in the summer as far as New England, looking for food plants. Their return migration occurs during the early dry season in Florida (October-November), when they may fly south in great numbers along the coast.

Appias drusilla neumoegenii. Range in Florida: southern tip of the mainland and the Florida Keys. Maximum wingspread: 2.5 inches. Months seen: every month. Caterpillar food: Capers

INTERESTING BUTTERFLY FACTS

1. Most butterflies have very different patterns on the top and bottom sides of their wings. This enables them to camouflage themselves by folding their wings so that only the bottom side is showing its usually dull pattern. However, when the butterfly needs to show a brilliant pattern, for example, when seeking a mate, all it needs to do is to open its wings.

2. Most butterflies bask in the sun in order to warm their bodies. They are cold-blooded, meaning that their bodies do not produce metabolic heat like human bodies do, so they must rely on the sun to raise their body temperature to the level where they can move about. On cold days they may not fly at all. Some butterfly species bask with their wings open and others with their wings shut, but aligned to catch the sun's rays.

3. Many butterflies are territorial and may fight with each other. Although they don't have weapons to really hurt each other in such skirmishes, the stronger, faster, butterflies manage to chase their weaker competitors out of their territory.

4. Most butterflies have a proboscis (pro-bahs-sis), a long tongue or feeding tube used to suck up liquid food such as flower nectar, and for sipping water. This tongue, when unrolled, can be as much as three times the length of the butterfly's body.

5. Butterflies start life by hatching from an egg as a caterpillar (also called a larva). When the caterpillar grows big enough, it wraps itself in a pupal case (also called a chrysalis) and changes (through a process called metamorphosis) into a butterfly. The butterfly completes its life cycle by finding a mate and laying eggs on a host plant which will provide food for the caterpillars.

6. There is a huge variety of butterflies and moths. There are more species of butterflies than of any other insect besides beetles.

7. Butterflies can see ultraviolet light which (although invisible to humans) makes many flower markings very striking and attractive. The ability to see ultraviolet light also helps some butterflies identify their own species when searching for a mate. These butterflies have ultraviolet reflectant or absorbant markings on their wings which are only visible to other butterflies.

△ The chrysalis of Pierid butterflies is distinct for its cone-shaped head (which is the top part of the hanging chrysalis). The chrysalis shown here is that of the Southern Dogface.

BUTTERFLY ATHLETES

Imagine a Cloudless Sulphur, fascinated, perhaps, by the myriad of brightly colored, bobbing sports logos, keeping pace with a large pack of runners in the Orlando Marathon. At the end of the race, the butterfly, which has had to contend with breezes not even noticed by the runners, still crosses the finish line much as it began, its entire expenditure of fuel and water weighing less than one smallish drop of sweat from the gasping humans. How can this butterfly display such strength and fuel efficiency? If it were the size of a Piper Cub airplane, would it really be able to circle the globe without stopping? The impressive strength and stamina of butterflies is an example of how scaling down to the size of a bug changes the whole world. As organisms increase in size, they become heavier much faster than they become stronger. This means that a man-sized cockroach might not be able to run any faster than a human, leaving aside the fact that the design of insects does not allow them to get that big. So small animals do very well in some situations, but not all. An ant may be able to carry 25 times its own weight, but we won't be hiring them on as stevedores, because the amazing weight they can carry is still only 25 times the weight of an ant. MD

Southern Dogface

The Southern Dogface, a highly specialized sulphur with a modified wing-shape, is seen around alfalfa and soybean fields in north Florida. The upperside of the wings is marked like a dog's face (some say a poodle), with heavy black margins. The leaf-shape and pattern on the underside help conceal the butterfly, especially when it is perched on a bush with yellow leaves. Note the rosy color along the veins on the underside of the Dogface's wings. This is especially prominent in the winter form. The forewings are a bit pointed.

Zerene cesonia. Wingspan: 2.5 inches. Range in Florida: enitre state. Caterpillar food: indigo bush, alfalfa, soybeans, white prairie clover. When seen: every month in southern Florida.

ANOTHER REASON TO LEARN ABOUT BUTTERFLIES

A child sent to school in a foreign country best knows the meaning of ignorance. What is the teacher saying? Is it important? What are the rules of the game they play around that tree at recess? This boy who is trying to talk to me, is he inviting me to kick the ball, or is he asking me where I got those strange shoes? It is a time of traumatic fear and loneliness.

Not long ago, almost everybody was brought up surrounded by the natural world. They recognized the creatures, though they might not know all their names, and they knew what was important, what was safe, what was fun to do or good to eat, how to play the games. This is no longer true. The human world is the only world in which many of us feel comfortable. This is especially the case in Florida, which becomes a home to many people late in life, so that much of what they learned elsewhere no longer seems to apply.

Even the children of Florida now tend to grow up indoors and are out in the open air only on city streets, mown playing fields, busy beaches, and screened porches. Nature may seem alien, weird, dangerous, or irrelevant. Our senses, which were tuned through our long history with nature, are denied the feelings, the smells, the visual complexity of the natural world. We somehow sense we should be out there enjoying the game but when we go out, we feel bored and lonely and return indoors to the television we know, which is always the same everywhere.

Butterflies are an invitation into the natural world and an introduction to the huge realm of insects, which seems particularly strange and threatening to many. But there is nothing scary about butterflies; indeed, their grace and agility, their colors and symmetry are almost impossible to resist. It is no wonder that so many scientists can trace the origin of their careers to an early fascination with butterflies. Butterflies are like the little girl with the shy smile who offers to teach a few important words of the new language. MD

NO TRAINING REQUIRED

Many of the complicated tasks performed by insects require no training, largely because nature often operates on the principle of do-it-right-the-first-time-or-die. When a caterpillar becomes a chrysalis, it sheds its skin one last time. Before shedding its skin, the caterpillar spins a small pad of silk on the surface where it will pupate. The chrysalis has a set of hooks on its rear end which it embeds in this pad of silk. The problem is for the limbless, blind chrysalis to emerge from the skin which is clinging to a vertical surface, and with quick writhing and jabbing movements, fasten the hooks of its rear into the tiny pad of silk before the old skin drops off the surface and before the chrysalis falls out of the skin. It's like changing out of clothing and into a sleeping bag, while hanging upside down, blindfolded. Those who miss fall to the ground and become food for ants.

MD

FACTS ABOUT SULPHER BUTTERFLIES:

1. Most sulphur females have a white form, and there are usually summer and winter forms for both sexes.

2. At rest, sulphurs fold their wings and rarely open them except for flight.

3. The large sulphurs are great migrants, flying hundreds of miles northward in the spring and southward in the fall.

BUTTERFLY ENVY

An early compendium of natural history information was put together by the Compte de Buffon (1707-1788), who expressed his envy of the butterfly condition thus: "The butterfly, to enjoy life, needs no other food but the dews of Heaven, and the honeyed juices that are distilled from every flower. The pageantry of princes cannot equal the ornaments with which it is invested, nor the rich color that embellishes its wings. The skies are the butterfly's proper habitation, and the air its element; whilst man comes into the world naked, and often roves about without habitation or shelter, exposed, on the one hand, to the heat of the sun, and on the other to the damps and exhalations of the earth, both alike enemies of his happiness and existence. A strong proof that, while this little animal is raised to its greatest height, we are as yet, in this world, only candidates for perfection!" MD

Family: Pieridae

Large Orange Sulphur

The Large Orange does not migrate to the same extent as the Cloudless Sulphur, so it is largely restricted to south Florida and the tropics. Males are almost pure orange above, while females have some darker markings.

Phoebis agarithe maxima. Range in Florida: South Florida and the Keys. When seen: entire year. Maximum wingspan: 2-3 inches. Caterpillar food: blackbead, cat's claw, wild tamarind.

▷ A female Large Orange Sulphur.

△ With its long tongue, the Large Orange Sulphur gets nectar from a variety of deep-throated flowers in the garden or in a natural habitat.

△ The caterpillar of the Large Orange Sulphur feeds on various species of Cassia. Like the adult, it is colorfully marked with yellow and black pigments.

Orange Sulphur

The Orange Sulphur, or Alfalfa Butterfly as it is sometimes called, is a highly variable butterfly, but there is almost always some orange pigment on the male and normal female. There are albino females as well. Although abundant throughout the United States, this butterfly becomes increasingly rare in Florida the farther south one goes. Only a few specimens have ever been seen in the Keys.

The genus name, *Colias*, is another name for Aphrodite, the goddess of love and beauty.

The Orange Sulphur feeds on many flowers as an adult. The dark green caterpillar is a pest on alfalfa in several states, but it is not abundant enough in Florida to cause significant harm.

Colias eurytheme. Range in Florida: mostly northern Florida, increasingly rare to the south. Maximum wingspread: 2.75 inches. Months seen: winter and early spring, usually. Caterpillar food: legumes, especially alfalfa and clover.

Sleepy Orange

Appropriately named, the male Sleepy Orange has a small, black, wavy line on the upperside of its forewing which resembles a half-closed eye. The sharply defined black border around its rich, orange-colored wings is also distinctive.

The underside of the adults varies from yellow-orange during the summer to brick red or brown during the winter. Its winter color helps camouflage it among dead leaves. The color change is initiated by changes in temperature and day length when the individuals are still caterpillars.

Eurema nicippe. Range in Florida: entire state. Months seen: all year. Maximum wingspread: 2.25 inches. Caterpillar food: legumes, especially cassias.

△ The Sleepy Orange occurs in two adult color forms. The winter form has a dark, orangish-brown underside which helps conceal it among dead leaves. This form is seen from November through February.

△ The summer color form of the Sleepy Orange butterfly has a yellowish underside. This form is seen from March to October.

THE ORIGIN OF THE WORD "BUTTERFLY"

The word "butterfly" was probably inspired by the buttery yellow color of the Brimstone, a very common European butterfly. The Brimstone is a relative of the sulphurs found in Florida and is one of the first European butterflies to appear in the spring.

Giant Orange Sulphur

Giant Sulphurs are frequent visitors to Spanish needles flowers along roadsides. The females differ from the males by having dark mottling on the top and undersides of their wings, while the males are mottled only on the undersides and are pure brilliant orange on top.

Phoebis agarithe. Range in Florida: South Florida. Caterpillar food: leaves and flowers of cassia trees.

Family: Pieridae

Orange-barred Sulphur

The Orange-barred Sulphur colonized Florida from the West Indies, with the first individuals arriving around 1928. Adults may have flown in or been blown in by a tropical storm. Another possibility is that larvae were brought in along with nursery plants. They soon became abundant, year-round residents of south Florida, probably because the larvae feed on a number of native shrubs in the genus *Cassia*, and adults could easily find these plants which grow wild throughout South Florida.

This is the largest sulphur butterfly in Florida. The distinctive males are bright yellow, with an orange patch across the front of the forewing and an orange border along the outer margin of the hindwings. Females are highly variable in color, ranging from white to yellow, but most have a reddish-orange border along the outer edge of the hindwings.

The adults have a swift and high flight, but they frequently visit red or yellow flowers to seek nectar. Urban areas and tropical pinelands near the host cassias are the best places to see this species.

Phoebis philea philea. Range in Florida: the southern half of the state, the Florida Keys, and occasionally north Florida. Maximum wingspread: 3 inches. Months seen: every month. Caterpillar food: legumes, especially cassias.

△ The male Orange-barred Sulphur (left) has orange bars on the upperside of its forewings. The female (right) has black markings along the edges of its wings.

△ The female Orange-barred Sulphur (left) has more dark markings on its underside than the male (right).

◁ The pupal case of the Orange-barred Sulphur becomes transparent before the adult emerges. The wing pattern of a male can be seen through the transparent casing. The pupa is suspended by a silk girdle.

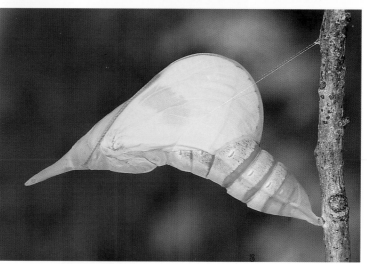

8

Barred Sulphur

This boldly marked species is one of Florida's most common butterflies. The male has a black bar along the trailing edge of the upperside of its forewings which the female lacks. Scent scales on this black bar emit a perfume that attracts females during courtship (see box on page 11).

The Barred Sulphurs which emerge in winter have darker wing colors. The normal satiny-white undersurface of the hindwing becomes brick red or tan. These darker colors may offer some protection when the species spends the winter in woodlands.

Like other sulphurs, this butterfly frequently migrates across extensive areas.

Eurema daira. Range in Florida: entire state. Maximum wingspread: 1 5/8 inches. Months seen: all year. Caterpillar food: legumes, especially pencil flower and joint vetch.

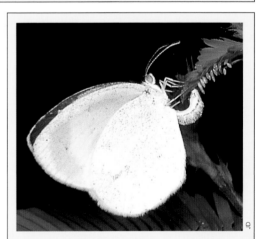

BUTTERFLY COLOR FORMS

This copulating pair of Barred Sulphurs shows how different seasonal color forms can be. The white butterfly is the summer form and the darker-colored butterfly is the fall form. Decreasing day length and falling temperatures trigger a change in the larvae that produces the darker winter form. This color helps conceal the butterflies among dead leaves in the woodlands where they spend the winter. Many species have these different color forms. However, they are never the same individuals. Butterflies do not change colors in the same manner as birds which molt their old feathers and grow new ones. A butterfly cannot molt its scales. Different colors belong to butterflies of different generations. But such color changes are not random. They help the butterfly survive in its changing environment.

THE DEADLY DINING ROOM

Caterpillars often leave their host plants and hastily travel some distance away before forming a pupa. For a caterpillar, there is no place more dangerous than the dining area. Easily trained enemies, such as birds and paper wasps, quickly make the association between a caterpillar and its host plant and can develop a targeting "search image" that enormously increases their ability to find that caterpillar. Worse yet, many of the most voracious enemies of caterpillars, such as the dreaded parasitic wasps and flies, are adept at tracking caterpillars by their spoor (droppings), the pattern of damage on a leaf, and the pungent, beckoning scent of shredded plant tissue that the caterpillar releases with every chomp of its jaws.

The poet Christina Rossetti (1830-1894) cast a sympathetic eye on a caterpillar racing away from one set of enemies through the gauntlet of another:

Brown and furry
Caterpillar in a hurry;
Take your walk
To the shady leaf or stalk.

May no toad spy you,
May the little birds pass by you,
Spin and die,
To live again a butterfly.

MD

OVIPOSITING: EGG-LAYING

Eggs are usually laid on the underside of leaves so as to be less noticeable. The female, in this case, a Barred Sulphur, curls her abdomen underneath her body and then under the leaf in order to attach the egg. Females identify the proper host plant visually and then double check their choice through sensory organs in their feet.

PUDDLING

Dozens or even hundreds of butterflies may be seen sipping moisture from ground soaked with animal urine or damp spots contaminated by dung or dead animals. But the purpose of puddling is probably not to obtain moisture. After all, dew is usually readily available and moist areas around streams are abundant in much of Florida. The places where butterflies are seen puddling are usually laden with minerals and salts that are needed by the butterflies.

Members of these "drinking clubs" or "puddling clubs" are almost exclusively males. During mating, the male loses a substantial amount of sodium and other salts in the sperm package which is transferred to the female. These minerals must be replenished before he can mate again. Common puddlers include several species of sulphurs, Tiger Swallowtails, and Red-spotted Purples.

△ A Cloudless Sulphur extending its proboscis into wet soil to drink

THE POET'S MISTAKE

Many poets have written about the attraction of butterflies to roses. For example:

Let me smell the wild rose
Sated from their blossoms rise
Honey bee and butterflies
                              Jean Ingelow

These poets have combined in their works the world's most popular flower with the world's most popular insect. However, they are scientifically misguided. Butterflies are not at all attracted to roses, as they do not supply nectar. Roses are designed to be pollinated by beetles which eat the abundant pollen held above the flower's base by thickets of stamens.

Schaus
swallowtail
butterfly

32 USA
1996

BUTTERFLY STAMPS

On October 2, 1996, the United States Postal Service issued fifteen endangered species stamps (32-cent commemoratives), one of which is the Schaus Swallowtail. Earlier, the USPS issued four 13-cent butterfly stamps, but none of these was a Florida butterfly.

BUTTERFLIES AS POLLINATORS

The relationship between flowers and butterflies is one of innocent sex and drinking: transport of pollen from the anther of one plant to the pistil of another is arranged with a fee of nectar. Butterflies are seldom as abundant as bees, nor do they visit flowers with such dedication, since bees are collecting groceries for the whole family, while butterflies are only refueling themselves. Butterflies, however, offer a peculiarly valuable function to plants: unlike bees, many butterflies travel long distances and thus may create a genetic link between farflung plants that home-based pollinators, such as bees, would never provide.

The continuation of genetic diversity in a species of plant may have great long-term importance for that species, though this would be difficult to prove without research programs of a scope and duration to boggle any funding agency. The cumulative importance of butterflies as pollinators is impossible to calculate because of the variable nature of butterfly excursions. As the great annual waves of butterflies sweep through Florida, they leave behind small ripples of enhanced genetic diversity.

As butterflies move more or less randomly across the landscape, looking for mates, or host plants for their offspring, they inadvertently arrange the marriages of plants from two isolated marshes, or from two patches of Florida scrub habitat. A small population of plants spread out over several acres may support several resident butterflies which have learned the location of each plant and visit them in turn.

We know of certain plants, such as the beautiful Florida scrub blazing star, and Curtis milkweed, that seem to be almost totally dependent on butterflies for pollination (both species are on the federal list of endangered species, which is why their pollination has been investigated). There must be many other butterfly-dependent plants that have not been studied. These straightforward relationships, however, are in the minority.

The true significance of butterflies as pollinators of native plants is as elusive as a Gulf Fritillary flying easily across some Florida river, leaving us with straining eyes and soaked shoes on the near shore. Butterflies of many species visit the daisy-like flowers of Spanish needles along Florida roadsides, but Kerri Schwarz of the University of Florida has shown that each transports only a tiny amount of pollen. However, this is seemingly enough to help improve genetic diversity and make Spanish needles a very successful weed.

MD

BUTTERFLY COURTSHIP

Mating rituals of butterflies are fascinating, and learning the behavior of each species is one of the most interesting activities of butterfly-watching. The basic function of an adult, male butterfly is to find a mate and copulate. The males of some species constantly patrol for females. The males of other species wait patiently on a perch and fly out to greet anything fluttering by which might be a female of their own kind. Sometimes, in their eagerness, they may even chase a leaf in the breeze, because their vision is not keen enough to make identification except at close range. However, one or both sexes are frequently equipped with scent glands which give off sexual perfumes (pheromones). These scents can be detected at a range of one mile or more in moths; it is not yet known at what range butterflies can detect these scents.

Once the male and female find each other, the male pursues the female. In some species this involves a spiraling flight upward. In most cases, when two or more butterflies are observed chasing each other, it is an

△ A pair of Julias copulating on a passionvine flower. The male is on the left.

attempted courtship flight rather than a territorial dispute. If the female is not impressed with her suitor, she will fly high enough to outdistance him and he will give up.

If there is mutual attraction, the male will fly above the female, wafting scent over her or even forcing her to the ground. There he may spread one or both wings above her and use the full impact of his scent glands to win her. Some species engage in elaborate routines in which the two butterflies stroke each other with their wings and antennae.

Once the pair begins copulation, they remain attached to each other for an average of 30 to 60 minutes (although the time can vary in different species from a few minutes to several hours). The joined pair may even fly together, although in this case, one butterfly actually carries the other along. In some species it is the male that carries the female, and in the others, the reverse.

△ This unusual photograph shows a Barred Sulphur male spreading its forewing to expose its scent glands directly above the female to induce her to mate.

The courtship of sulphur butterflies usually begins with the male flying above the female and encouraging her to land. After the female lands, the male may flutter above her, touching her occasionally, and finally releasing his pheromone (a chemical sexual stimulant) from his scent glands as shown in the photo.

The sequence just described occurs when the female is willing to mate. Frequently she is not, and usually the reason is that she has already mated. In this case, she will fly upwards in a spiral path with the male following her until he tires and gives up the chase. Female sulphurs may sometimes be white in color, although white females are more common in the northern states.

AN AMAZING KNOWLEDGE OF BUTTERFLIES

There are about 160 species of butterflies in Florida. That's a lot of names to learn. Many of these species, however, are seldom seen because they occur in only a few places in Florida, or are generally rare, or spend most of their time up in the tops of trees. There is a much smaller number of species that appear regularly: a few sulphurs, a few swallowtails, a few hairstreaks, brushfoots and milkweed butterflies, a wood satyr or two, and some of the more distinctive skippers. It's easier to learn butterflies than birds. But with most groups of animals, there are some confusing sets of similar species; the

many skippers can be as frustrating to tell apart as winter sandpipers. This book is designed to showcase the common and distinctive species of butterflies. With a little practice, the names of butterflies will fall casually from the amateur naturalist's lips. While leaning back in a garden chair, gazing out over the zinnias, and not totally unaware of the surprised and admiring glances of friends, he might say, "That's a Palamedes Swallowtail, whose caterpillar lives on red bay and looks like a small snake. And that's a Long-tailed Skipper, which may have just flown down from Georgia last week." MD

Family: Pieridae

Cloudless Sulphur

Most Floridians are familiar with this beautiful butterfly, which is called "cloudless" because the male is pure yellow without any markings on the upperside of its wings. Starting around the first of September, millions of males and females migrate south through the state to the southern counties and, in many cases, onward across the Gulf of Mexico.

Cloudless Sulphurs may be seen crossing highways and fields, and even flying over tall buildings, in their haste to move ever onward. They are often noticed on golf courses and at daytime track meets and other field events. Cloudless Sulphurs are regularly seen drifting across the field at the University of Florida stadium during home football games from September through November, the period of their extended southward migration. A similar migration, but smaller and less noticeable, occurs in a northward direction in the spring.

A small number of adults spend the winter in northern Florida in the woods, hiding in undergrowth and resting quietly during December and January, becoming active only on the warmest days.

Phoebus sennae. Range in Florida: entire state. Maximum wingspread: 3 inches. Months seen: all year. Caterpillar foods: cassias.

△ The male Cloudless Sulphur is an evenly colored, bright yellow on its upper wings, while the female has mottling along the edges and underside of its wings.

▽ The Cloudless Sulphur, one of the most common butterflies in Florida, migrates through the state in huge numbers each spring and fall.

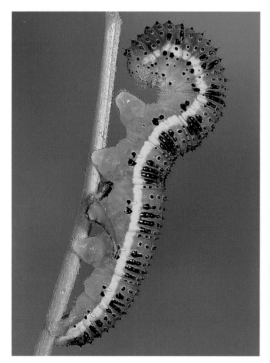

△ The caterpillar of the Cloudless Sulphur has tiny bumps on its body and a bright yellow stripe along each side. These markings help the caterpillar avoid detection by birds and other predators by breaking up the body's outline. This coloration also blends well with the cassia plants upon which this caterpillar feeds.

◁ This tattered Cloudless Sulphur drinks from a flower while a hummingbird waits its turn. Cloudless Sulphur butterflies visit many flowers, including some deep-throated red flowers that are normally visited by hummingbirds. (This photo was not staged.)

Dainty Sulphur

This is the smallest Florida sulphur, and as tiny as this butterfly is, it is hard to believe that each year it migrates from Florida to the northeastern states and from the southwestern United States to Washington, Minnesota, and even central Canada. In Florida, it is one of the most common butterflies. Unlike most sulphurs which use legumes as host plants, the Dainty Sulphur caterpillar feeds on members of the aster family, especially marigolds and Spanish needles.

This butterfly's color pattern is very similar to that of the somewhat larger Barred Sulphur, and some biologists think there may be a mimicry complex involving these and related sulphur species. It is not yet known if they are distasteful to birds or lizards. The hindwing of the summer form is pale yellow on the underside of the adult, while that of the winter form is dusky green. Adults are quiet on cold winter days but become active as soon as the temperature warms up to a reasonable level.

Nathalis iole. Range in Florida: entire state. Maximum wingspread: 1.25 inches. Months seen: all year. Caterpillar food: aster family members such as Spanish needles.

△ A Dainty Sulphur feeding on Spanish needles (*Bidens*).

△ A Dainty Sulphur perched on southern fleabane. This small butterfly migrates great distances during summer, from southern Florida up to the northeastern states.

Little Sulphur

Another of the small sulphur species, the Little Sulphur strays north from Florida and Texas each summer and temporarily colonizes much of eastern North America, including southern Canada. In Florida, it prefers dry, sandy fields and roadside areas where its larval food plant, cassia, grows abundantly. The male is always yellow with a broad black tip on the forewing and a black border around the hindwing. The female may be yellow or white, with only a small black patch on the border of the hindwing.

Eurema lisa. Range in Florida: entire state. Maximum wingspread: 1.75 inches. Months seen: every month. Caterpillar food: partridge pea.

▷ The Little Sulphur, like other Florida sulphurs, has both summer and winter forms. The winter form of this species (shown here) is a bit more tan but is not much darker than the summer form.

△ The whitish summer form of the Little Sulphur.

13

Gossamer-winged Butterflies

Family: Lycaenidae
Subfamily: Hairstreaks

Hairstreaks are usually small butterflies with delicate wings. All have wingspans of less than two inches. Most have brilliant metallic colors on the uppersides of their wings. Their antennae are distinctively marked with delicate rings. Males usually have only two pairs of well-developed legs, capable of walking, although in the females, all three pairs are completely developed. Most hairstreaks have "tails" extending from their hindwings. Many of the caterpillars of blues and hairstreaks have honey glands which are milked by ants. The ants, in return, provide some protection against enemies such as wasps.

Gray Hairstreak

The Gray Hairstreak occurs throughout the United States and is the most widespread and commonly seen hairstreak butterfly in Florida. Adults can be found foraging for nectar on many different flowers in open fields or along woodland edges. The larva of the Gray Hairstreak is the Cotton Square Borer which eats young cotton buds and causes damage. It also damages bean and corn crops.

Strymon melinus. Range in Florida: entire state. Maximum wingspread: 1.2-1.4 inches. Months seen: February through November. Caterpillar food: legumes.

▷ A Gray Hairstreak male with its wings open, feeding on blackroot flowers. Dark scent-scales in the center of each forewing are visible in this photo. The male emits a scent from these glands to attract females.

△ A Gray Hairstreak sipping nectar from deep inside a lantana flower. Note the thin hairline markings on this butterfly which, along with the hairlike tail projections, inspire its name.

In many species of hairstreaks, the tail looks like a head. Scientists call this "front-to-back mimicry." The spots at the back of the wings resemble eyes and the long, tail-like wing extensions look like antennae.

The white markings on the "tails" make them very conspicuous. All this deception encourages predators to attack the tail, thus increasing the butterfly's chance of escaping with its life.

The hairstreak's habit of feeding and perching with its head down while waving the antennae-like tail projections in the air reinforces its camouflage by making its tail seem even more like a head.

BUTTERFLY WORDS

There are special words to describe the life cycle of butterflies and moths. The butterfly or moth is actually the mature adult (sometimes called the imago). There are three earlier immature stages: egg, caterpillar, or pupa. The egg hatches to become the larva, which is also called a caterpillar. Caterpillars go through a series of molts, shedding their external skeleton or skin repeatedly, and each stage between molts is called an instar. The stage which follows the larva and precedes the adult is the pupa. Many moths and some butterfly caterpillars spin a silken-thread cocoon around themselves before they turn into a pupa. This cocoon helps protect the pupa from predators, parasites, and the weather. For butterflies, the naked pupa is also called a chrysalis. While the insect is in the pupa stage, it transforms itself from caterpillar to moth or butterfly through a process called complete metamorphosis.

Great Purple Hairstreak

This butterfly should more properly be called the Great Blue Hairstreak, because the wings of the males are a rich royal blue rather than purple on the uppersides (another hairstreak, in Colorado, has true purple uppersides). Nevertheless, the common name, Great Purple, has stuck to Florida's blue hairstreak species. The undersides of the wings are deep blackish gray, with only a hint of bluish purple along the leading edge of the forewing. The adults visit garden flowers readily and are often seen in urban areas.

Atlides halesus. Range: south-central Florida northward through the Panhandle and west to California. Maximum wingspread: 1.3-2 inches. Caterpillar food: mistletoe, a parasitic plant that grows on tree branches.

▷ The Great Purple Hairstreak, the largest North American hairstreak, is found in scattered colonies throughout Florida. The larvae feed on mistletoe.

△ The slug-like caterpillar of the Great Purple Hairstreak feeds on mistletoe.

△ The Great Purple Hairstreak has the finest iridescent blue of any Florida butterfly. The bright blue patch at the base of its forewing is often covered by the hindwing.

Red-banded Hairstreak

The Red-banded Hairstreak is named after the distinctive red-orange line on its hindwings. The uppersides of the wings are dusky blue. This small hairstreak butterfly is remarkably abundant throughout the southeastern United States in the edges of woods, overgrown fields, and coastal hardwood hammocks. It can be seen year-round in the woodlands of Florida.

The eggs are laid on the fallen leaves of sumacs, oaks, and wax myrtle. The larvae crawl up nearby tree trunks and feed on the living leaves of these same species.

Calycopis cecrops. Range in Florida: entire state. Maximum wingspread: one inch. Months seen: all year. Caterpillar food: leaves of oaks, sumac, and wax myrtle.

◁ A Red-banded Hairstreak feeding on a goldenrod flower.

Gossamer-winged Butterflies

Family: Lycaenidae
Subfamily: Hairstreaks

Bartram's Hairstreak

Bartram's Hairstreak was named after William Bartram, a famous naturalist who explored Florida in the eaarly 1700s and wrote about his travels. It occurs in south Florida in openings in pine forests where its larval food plant, the native woolly croton, grows. The orange eyespot on the underside, at the base of the two tails, is quite large and conspicuous. This butterfly has at times been proposed for a listing on the Federal Endangered Species Act, although currently it seems to be common enough not to need that protection.

Strymon acis bartrami. Range in Florida: South Florida and the Florida Keys. Maximum wingspread: 1 inch. Months seen: all year. Caterpillar food: woolly croton.

White-M Hairstreak

This unusual butterfly has a white, black-edged line in the middle of the hindwing that forms a white "M" (or "W"). It flies throughout the eastern United States and prefers wooded areas in Florida. This same hairstreak also travel south through Mexico and as far as Venezuela. Some of its relatives occur in the mountains of Central and South America. Its larval food plants are various species of oaks. The pupa is hidden among oak leaf litter at the base of the host tree. The pupa can wriggle and when it does so, it may produce squeaking noises.

Parrhasius m-album. Range in Florida: entire state. Maximum wingspread: 1.2-1.6 inches. Months seen: February to November. Generations per year: four. Caterpillar food: leaves of oaks.

Sweadner's Hairstreak

Sweadner's Hairstreak, also called the St. Augustine Hairstreak, feeds only on southern red cedar trees in the northern and middle part of Florida, especially along the coasts where these trees are more numerous. Its bright green undersides with reddish and white bands and elongated spots will readily distinguish this hairstreak from others in Florida. The larvae are flat and slug-like, bright green and white in color, and they perfectly match the conelike scales of the cedar trees. Adults may be seen visiting small flowers along roadsides and trails. This butterfly was long thought to be a subspecies of the more northern Olive Hairstreak but is now considered a distinct species.

Mitoura sweadneri. Range: northern and central Florida, particularly along coastal areas. Maximum wingspread: 1 inch. Months seen: March to November. Generations per year: at least three. Caterpillar food: southern red cedar.

Atala Butterfly

The Atala stands out as one of Florida's most beautiful and colorful insects. It features the metallic blue that is typical of hairstreak butterflies from tropical regions. Hairstreaks found farther north in the United States generally lack this feature and are much duller in appearance. Florida is the northernmost range of these tropical butterflies.

The Atala is found in tropical pinelands and hardwood habitats in close association with the caterpillar's main foodplant, a native cycad called coontie (*Zamia pumila*). The adults fly very slowly and males frequently perch on the leaves of shrubs, watching for female Atalas to fly through their areas. Both sexes often visit flowers.

Large-scale harvesting of coontie for starch (sometimes called arrowroot starch) during the late 1800s greatly reduced the number of host plants, and the Atala dropped in numbers on the southern mainland. Development of the coastal habitats that were favored by the Atala also had a tremendous impact, and the species nearly became extinct. By 1965 there was only one known colony.

Dedicated conservationists provided coontie plants for the few remaining butterflies to lay their eggs and then moved the potted plants with the eggs to various locations to start new colonies. Their efforts were successful, and, since about 1980, the Atala has made a spectacular recovery. It is now found throughout urban and natural areas from Miami north to Fort Lauderdale, including the Everglades National Park.

Eumaeus atala florida. Range in Florida: southern tip of the mainland. Maximum wingspread: 1.6-2 inches. Months seen: all year. Caterpillar foods: coontie, a cycad species.

△ The red-orange abdomen warns potential predators that this butterfly is toxic. Its larval foodplant, a cycad, contributes poisonous compounds that are carried by the adults. Both males and females have the bright-red abdomen. Note also the striking red patch on the hindwing (near the abdomen).

△ The upperside of both the male and female Atala butterfly is black. The male (shown here) has soft, iridescent blue-green scaling. Females, on the other hand, have a streak of blue along the margin of the forewing.

Note that the Atala, unlike most other hairstreaks, does not have small "tails" extending from its hind wings. Compare to the Bartram's Hairstreak (previous page).

◁ Atala caterpillars are bright red in color with yellow spots. In addition to the native coontie, these caterpillars feed on a large number of exotic cycads. They sometimes trouble homeowners in the Fort Lauderdale and Miami areas when they become abundant on the exotic cycads which are frequently used in landscaping.

17

Gossamer-winged Butterflies

Family: Lycaenidae
Subfamily: Blues

Blues are among the smallest butterflies. Male members of this group frequently have iridescent blue on the upperside of their wings although they may be whitish underneath. Females are not as colorful. Note also the rounded shape of the wings.

Ceraunus Blue

The Ceraunus Blue is also called the Antillian Blue and the Florida Blue. It is often found where land has been disturbed by man and also in tropical pinelands, especially from the Keys to as far north as Central Florida. To the north, this species is more sporadic in distribution but still common.

Hemiargus ceraunus. Range: entire state, more common in the southern half. Maximum wingspread: 0.7-1.2 inches. Months seen: every month in the Keys; warmer months only to the north. Caterpillar food: various legumes, including indigo bush.

△▽ The Ceraunus Blue is one of the most common blues in Florida. The male (below and lower left) is bright blue on the upperside, while the female (above) is mostly brown.

The large eyespot at the outer edge of the hindwing in the photo above probably serves to attract a pursuing bird's attention to the less-vulnerable wing area, away from the head and body. The butterfly can easily afford to lose a bit of the hindwing, especially if the alternative is its head!

The black and white bands around the antennae are a noticeable feature of all the butterflies in this family. (Some of the Nymphalids also have these bands.)

Spring Azure Blue

This is often the first butterfly seen in spring in northern Florida when the azaleas are in full bloom. It is found as far south as Gainesville in low numbers. Similar species are found all across North America.

Adult Spring Azure Blues feed on flowering dogwoods, azaleas and other plants that bloom in early spring. The caterpillars feed on flowers of various forest shrubs. A succession of broods comes out during the spring, summer, and fall. The pure light blue color of the upper wings of the males is striking.

Identification of Spring Azure Blues is sometimes difficult. There are some closely related species (called sibling species) in which the adults are almost identical to the adult Spring Azure Blues. In such cases, differences in the larvae must be examined for accurate indentification.

Celastrina argiolus. Range in Florida: extreme northern Florida down to Gainesville. Maximum wingspread: 1-1.3 inches. Months seen: March to September. Caterpillar food: flowers of forest shrubs and small trees.

Eastern Pygmy Blue

One of the smallest butterflies in the world, the Eastern Pygmy Blue is very inconspicuous as it flutters low over coastal plains and the edges of tidal marshes in Florida. The larvae usually feed on glasswort, a plant of the salt marshes.

Brephidium isophthalma. Range: northeastern coast of Florida, and Gulf coast from the Big Bend area to Key West. Maximum wingspread: 0.7-0.9 inches. Months seen: every month. Caterpillar food: glassworts and saltworts.

POETS OF THE BLUES

The poet, Keats, rhapsodized over the small size of the blues:

"Little bright-eyed things that float through the air on azure wings."

Robert Frost was also taken with the blues. Calling them "skyflakes," he wrote:

"It is a blue-butterfly day here in spring,
And with these sky-flakes down in flurry on flurry,
There is more unmixed color on the wing,
Than flowers will show for days, unless they hurry."

Cassius Blue

The Cassius Blue is a very common species throughout Florida except in the Panhandle. The adults fly along the edges of tropical hardwood hammocks and tropical pinelands, along beaches, and in weedy fields and other disturbed sites.

Leptotes cassius theonus. Range: Throughout Florida except Panhandle. Maximum wingspread: 0.75-1.2 inches. Months seen: every month in south Florida; summer only to the north. Caterpillar food: flowers of wild legumes, including trees.

19

Gossamer-winged Butterflies

Family: Lycaenidae
Subfamily: Metalmarks

The subfamily name, metalmarks, refers to the metallic markings found on the wings of many of the species. In North America, metalmarks tend to be less brilliant than in the tropics.

Little Metalmark

The Little Metalmark is a tiny, brownish-orange butterfly with various markings of metallic bluish-gray. It is the only metalmark species in Florida. Favored habitats include grassy areas in open, sandy, pine woodland.

Calephelis virginiensis. Range: entire state of Florida. Maximum wingspread: 0.5-1 inches. Months seen: mid-March to mid-October. Caterpillar food: thistles.

△ The Little Metalmark, Florida's only metalmark butterfly, is a member of a family which reaches remarkable diversity in the Central and South American tropics, with over 1,300 species named so far.

The Little Metalmark gets its common name from the metallic gold and blue specks on its copper-colored wings.

Snout Butterflies

Family: Libytheidae

Bachman's Snout Butterfly

Bachman's Snout Butterfly can be immediately distinguished from all other Florida butterflies by the very long snout projecting forward from its head. This snout is composed of two "palpi" (special structures that look like small brushes) on either side of the proboscis. It is a member of the longbeak family.

This butterfly uses its snout as part of its camouflage. The wings resemble a dead leaf and the snout looks like the stem. When at rest on a branch with its head is down, its snout resembles a stem attaching the leaf to the branch. The forewings are considerably longer than the hindwings and have an unusual, squared shape.

This butterfly is found throughout much of the eastern United States. It belongs to a small family of about a dozen species worldwide, with only one species, usually, on each continent. Several species are restricted to oceanic islands. In the southwestern part of the United States, this butterfly has been known to migrate in such huge numbers as to darken the sky.

Libytheana bachmanii. Range in Florida: mainland Florida; more common in the northern part of the state. Maximum wingspread: 1.7-2 inches. Months seen: June to November. Caterpillar food: leaves of hackberry trees.

ULTRAVIOLET LIGHT

Ultraviolet light is abundant in daylight, but it is invisible to human eyes. However, butterflies are capable of seeing the ultraviolet end of the light spectrum. Many flowers which are pollinated by butterflies and other insects have taken advantage of this fact by developing patterns which are visible only to an insect that can see ultraviolet light. Thus, flowers such as impatiens and a number of other broad-petalled flowers have areas on their rim which appear bright in ultraviolet light, because they reflect UV light, while the center parts of the flower petals absorb UV light and appear dark or black.

To an approaching butterfly, the dark markings provide "honey guides" that enable the butterfly to land at the center of the flower and to quickly find and insert its tongue in the small opening of the floral tube located there. The butterfly benefits by being able to minimize its time spent hovering or crawling over a flower. By drawing up the nectar in the shortest possible time, it also lessens its exposure to passing predators such as birds and

△ *A daisy in normal daylight. The center of the flower is rather even, both in brightness and in color.*

△ *In ultraviolet light, the ripe, nectar-filled florets at the daisy's center show bright sparkles which guide the butterfly in to feed.*

lizards. The butterfly is far more vulnerable when feeding then when in flight.

The flower benefits by having a special attractiveness to butterflies. In its competition with plants that have more brightly colored flowers, a flower with UV visible markings may gain the upper hand in attracting butterflies

and thus get pollinated. For this reason, thousands of years of natural selection have enabled certain plants to develop nectar guides which are visible to the ultraviolet-sensitive eyes of insects such as butterflies.

CULTURAL SYMBOLISM OF BUTTERFLIES AND MOTHS

Throughout history, moths have been related in folklore to spirits of the dead. However, to the Chinese in Southeast Asia, moths are more than just symbols of the soul. Most houses in this region do not have window screens. If a moth should fly through a window into a house and the day happens to be the anniversary of the death of a family member, the moth will be welcomed and, for sure, will not be chased away or killed. It would be regarded as the spirit of the departed person returning in another form for a visit. To millinons of Southeast Asian Chinese, this is not just folklore, but a firmly held belief.

The butterfly in Asia symbolizes a man who goes from woman to woman in the manner that a butterfly goes from flower to flower. A woman worried about her partner's fidelity might say "I cannot marry this guy. For sure, he will butterfly on me." The comparison is not restricted to men. Some Asian prostitutes wear butterfly jewelry as a symbol of their profession.

Although the ancient Greeks viewed butterflies as departed souls, for the most

part butterflies have been seen in a manner quite different from moths. While moths are mostly creatures of the night, the mostly day-flying butterflies have been regarded as symbols of freedom, and have appeared on tombstones as symbols of rebirth. The amazing transformation of a caterpillar into a butterfly through metamorphosis gives rise to much of this mysterious folklore.

Butterflies do not appear in the Bible, perhaps because of their relative scarcity in the dry climates of the Middle East. However, moths are mentioned as symbols of destruction. For example, in Mathew 6:19, Jesus says in his famous Sermon on the Mount, "Lay not up for yourselves treasures upon earth, where moth and rust doth corrupt, and where theives break through and steal…"

In Mexico, butterflies have been used as symbols of the sun and of fire. Flames rising around human sacrifices were described as flights of butterflies.

The French refer to depressing thoughts as papillons noirs, black butterflies.

THE NOVELIST AND THE BUTTERFLIES

One of this century's greatest writers was also one of the most passionate butterfly lovers of all time. Vladimir Nabokov, the author of "Lolita" and many other acclaimed works, was also a gifted entomologist. He declared his passionate love of butterflies in many of his writings.

"Literature and butterflies are the two sweetest passions known to man."

"Through the smells of the bog, I caught the subtle perfume of butterfly wings on my fingers, a perfume which varies with the species—vanilla, or lemon or musk, or a musty sweetish odor difficult to define. Still unsated, I pressed forward."

"…the highest enjoyment of timelessness—in a landscape selected at random—is when I stand among rare butterflies and their food plants …a thrill of gratitude to whom it may concern…to tender ghosts humoring a lucky mortal."

THE WORD "BUTTERFLY" IN MANY LANGUAGES

It may be just a coincidence, but it seems that the word for butterfly in many languages has a beautiful, interesting, or rhythmic sound. Double sounds are especially common perhaps because of the repetitive beats of a butterfly's wings. Here are a few samples (some spelled phonetically):

Spanish: *Mar-i-po'-sa*
French: *Papillon*
Portuguese: *Borboleta*
German: *Schmetterling*
Italian: *Farfalla*
Greek: *Petalutha*
Arabic: *Farrash*
Hebrew: *Parpar*
Russian: *Bah'-bohch-ka*

Samoan: *Pepe*
Norwegian: *Sommerfugl*
Swahili: *Kipepeo*
Chinese: *Hoo'-dee-eh*
Japanese: *Cho-cho*
Malay: *Rama rama*
Tagalog: *Paru-paro*
Cebuano: *Alibangbang*
Thai: *Pee-soo'-ah*

Korean: *Nah-bee*
Dutch: *Vlinder*
Tamil: *Vannathi poochi*
Irish: *Faylicon*
Burmese: *Lake-ti-ya*
Vietnamese: *Boom*
Hawaiian: *Pulelehua*
Nigerian: *Laba-laba*
Hungarian: *Pillango*

Brush-footed Butterflies

Family: Nymphalidae
Subfamily: Heliconiinae

The front pair of legs of both male and female brush-footed butterflies are small and not useful for walking, so these butterflies walk about on only four of their legs. The small, first pair of legs is covered with brush-like scales; hence the family name, brush-footed.

These small legs also contain sensors for chemicals found in leaves and flowers. The female uses these brushes to scrape the surface of plant leaves to confirm chemically that she has found the proper plant before laying her eggs. The brushes may also be used for cleaning the eyes, but this behavior has only been observed a few times.

Brush-footed butterflies have antennae with rather large knobs, and they perch with their wings partially open. Most brush-footed butterflies fly in a zig-zag path, probably to avoid predators. The very large Nymphalid family includes butterflies of a great variety of sizes and colors. The chrysalises of this group hang from the tip (which is attached to a silk pad) and do not employ a silk girdle. Their caterpillars generally have spines.

There are two subfamilies of brush-footed butterflies in Florida: the True Nymphalines and the Heliconians. In Florida, the Heliconians include the Julia, the Gulf Fritallary and the Zebra Longwing.

Julia

The fast-flying Julia is also called the Orange Longwing. It is a member of a group of tropical butterflies of Central and South America that ranges up into southern and occasionally Central Florida. The name Julia is a corruption of the species name, *iulia*. The genus name, *Dryas*, refers to the legendary Greek Dryads who were beautiful tree nymphs. The sun-loving, tropical Julia butterfly is commonly seen in the company of Gulf Fritillaries and the Zebra Longwings in South Florida and the Florida Keys.

Dryas iulia. Range in Florida: the Florida Keys to much of central Florida. Maximum wingspread: 3.2-3.8 inches. Months seen: every month in South Florida; summer months only in Central Florida. Caterpillar foods: passionflower vines.

△ The photo above shows a pair of Julia butterflies mating. The male on the left can be recognized by its brighter color. Butterflies mate in this back to back position and are vulnerable to predators while attached to each other because they cannot disengage quickly or easily. They can still fly; however, one must carry the other.

It is clear from this photo that these brush-footed butterflies are standing on two pairs of legs. The other pair of legs has been modified to a small, brush-like shape and is hardly noticeable.

▽ Note the long, narrow shape of the Julia's wings, which is typical of heliconians.

△ Passionvine is a primary food source for heliconian butterflies. The Julia looks a bit like a Gulf Fritillary with its wings open, but, unlike the Gulf Fritillary, the Julia does not have silver spots under its wings

THE UNIQUE HELICONIANS (LONGWINGS)

In Florida, the Heliconians include the Julia, the Gulf Fritillary, and the Zebra Longwing. The members of this subfamily of brush-footed butterflies are warm-weather butterflies that cannot survive the cold of northern states. Gulf Fritillaries are sometimes seen in the north in summer; they migrate northward in the warm summer months and then back to the south.

Heliconians have the unusual feeding technique of collecting pollen on their proboscis (see page 25).

All the butterflies of this group are attracted to passion-flowers. Chemicals in the passion-flower vines which are consumed by the longwing caterpillars give both the caterpillars and the adults a bad taste, giving them some measure of protection from predators.

Zebra Longwings, which roost together (see page 25), not only taste bad to predators, they also smell bad. The combined odor of a large number of Zebras roosting together may help advertise their distasteful properties.

△ The colorful patterns of the Julia caterpillar advertise the fact that it tastes bad. It incorporates distasteful compounds from the passionflower vines on which it feeds, thus protecting itself from predators during this stage. The butterflies also retain some of these bad-tasting chemicals. Note the white spots and the light-colored head which are the distinctive markings of this caterpillar.

◁ To potential predators, the twisted and convoluted pupa of the Julia looks very much like a twisted, dead leaf, or a piece of tree bark.

Brush-footed Butterflies

Family: Nymphalidae
Subfamily: Heliconiinae

Zebra Longwing

In 1996, the Zebra Longwing was proclaimed the official Florida State butterfly. This distinctive black butterfly with narrow yellow stripes is unique among Florida species due to its long narrow wings and slow, hovering flight. The adults breed all year in southern Florida and spread northward each spring. Their favored habitat in the southern tip of Florida is tropical hammocks; in northern Florida they may be seen in moist woods and along the edges of pine forests. At night, the adults roost in clusters numbering from a half dozen to 60 or more, and they return to the same roost night after night for weeks or even months. Individual adults may live as long as 4 to 6 months in the wild.

This butterfly goes through many generations a year because its life cycle from egg to adult can be as short as 21 days. The caterpillar is creamy white, with many fine crossbands of black and six rows of branched, black spines. These spines do not sting.

A good place to see Zebra Longwing butterflies is the hammocks of the Everglades. It is most often seen in South Florida but may also be found as far north as Gainesville and Tallahassee in the fall.

Note the rosy-pink patch on the tip of the lower hind wing of the Zebra.

Heliconius charitonius. Range in Florida: entire state. Maximum wingspread: 2.8-4.0 inches. Months seen: every month in South Florida, summer and fall to the north. Caterpillar food: passion-flower vine.

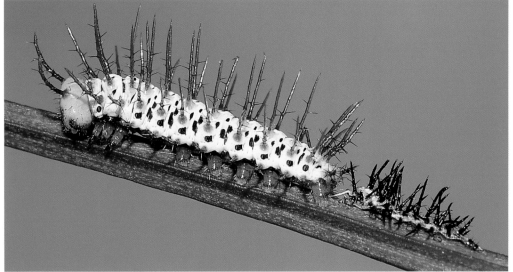

△ This Zebra caterpillar has just shed its skin, in a manner similar to that of a snake. This is the only way caterpillars can grow. The old skin is separated from the body by a digestive molting fluid. Each stage is called an instar. When scientists refer to a particular stage of caterpillar growth, they may refer, for example, to the "fifth instar." In some species, caterpillars go through as many as nine instars. The Zebra caterpillar molts five times before it pupates.

Notice the color of the new spines. They will soon turn solid black like the ones on the shed skin.

△ In this photo, two Zebra males have landed on the pupa of a female and are waiting for her to emerge so that they can mate with her. Males can detect the scent of a female within her pupa before she emerges, and a number of males may congregate. The males will literally fight with each other for the opportunity of mating with the female as soon as she breaks the pupal skin. The fastest, strongest male will prevail. This behavior has been called "pupal rape," since the female may be too weak immediately after emerging to effectively resist. "Rape" may not be an accurate description, because the female may be consenting. But, this would be difficult to determine. In some cases the males can gain entry to the pupal case and then do not even wait for the female to emerge. They mate with her inside the case. After mating, the successful male applies a chemical which acts as a repellant to other males. This helps ensure that the offspring will carry only the genes of the first male.

△ An adult Zebra butterfly drinking nectar from the flowers of Spanish needles. Note the long, narrow shape of the Zebra wings.

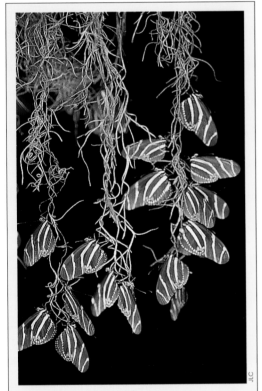

A SOCIAL BUTTERFLY

Zebra Longwings have several habits which are unusual among butterflies. For one thing, Zebras are remarkably social animals. At night, the butterflies roost together in groups of up to 60 individuals. In the late afternoon, both male and female Zebras fly from all points of the compass to their roost and hang motionless on a single stem or branch. They return to this same roost night after night.

EXTERNAL DIGESTION

This close-up view of a Zebra Longwing shows pollen sticking to the outside of its coiled proboscis (its tongue or feeding tube). Compare the proboscis in this photo to the proboscis in the photo at the top of the opposite page.

Most butterflies in Florida drink nectar from a variety of plants, but Zebras and other Heliconian butterflies also feed on pollen. In the mid-morning hours, they visit flowers with sticky pollen and collect the pollen in globs on the outside of their proboscis.

After a butterfly gathers a ball of pollen in this manner, it sits quietly on a sheltered leaf for an hour or more while it secretes digestive enzymes through the tip of its proboscis onto the ball of pollen. The enzymes break down the protein of the pollen grains into amino acids which the butterfly then sucks up through its proboscis. These amino acids are used to produce sperm or eggs as well as for general body maintenance.

This daily "external digestion" of pollen is a important source of nutrition and helps explain why Zebras live for up to five or six months as adults, much longer than most other butterflies whose lifespan may be only a few weeks.

This photo also shows how the first pair of legs has been reduced to tiny, brush-like structures. This unusual adaptation is the source of the family name, brush-footed butterflies. Although the tiny legs are of no use for supporting the weight of the butterfly, they contain sensors which help the butterfly identify food plants for its larvae.

Brush-footed Butterflies

Family: Nymphalidae
Subfamily: Heliconiinae

Gulf Fritillary

With its bright orange uppersides, and iridescent silver spots on the underside of its wings, this butterfly cannot be mistaken for any other in Florida. It is named after the colorful, orange-red fritillary flower. The reference to the Gulf is due to the fact that this species is common in the states around the Gulf of Mexico.

This species cannot survive freezing temperatures at any stage of its life. It flies all year in southern Florida and recolonizes northern Florida after cold winters. Its habitat is much the same as that of the Zebra: woodland edges, city gardens, and open, brushy fields where the adults avidly visit lantana flowers. (However, Zebras prefer to have the shade of a few trees).

Agraulis vanillae. Range in Florida: entire state. Maximum wingspread: 2.5-3.8 inches. Months seen: all year in South Florida, June to December in North Florida if there are hard freezes. Caterpillar food: passion-flower vines.

△ This Gulf Fritillary is sipping nectar from a thistle. Some specimens of Gulf Fritillaries have dark areas on their wings. These butterflies are said to be melanistic.

△ The Gulf Fritillary Butterfly is beautifully patterned on the underside, with shining silver spots across both wings and a rich rose patch at the base of the forewing. The brown and red areas have pigmented scales, while the color of the silver spots is created when light is refracted through prisms in the wing scales.

△ The upperside of the Gulf Fritillary is rich orange in the male and a slightly duller brown in the female. The Gulf Fritillary is one of the most common butterflies in Florida. Because its larvae feed on passion-vine, the adults are presumed to be distasteful to birds.

△ As a butterfly ages, its wings become increasingly torn. Most butterflies continue to fly until approximately half of either wing is gone.

△ The Gulf Fritillary caterpillar is shiny black, with reddish-orange stripes on its top and sides and four rows of spines which are harmless to humans.

THE GULF FRITILLARY IS NOT A TRUE FRITILLARY

The Gulf Fritillary, although it is one of Florida's three longwing (heliconian) butterflies, is a bit different from the Julia and the Zebra. Its wings are not as long, and it feeds only on nectar, not on pollen. However, scientifically, it is still considered a longwing and not a true fritillary.

True fritillaries (which are only relatives of the longwings) are also orange in color and have silver spots on the underside of their hindwings, but they have more rounded forewings and hence a more compact appearance. True fritillaries, in the genus Speyeria, only occur north and west of Florida, in the cooler areas of North America.

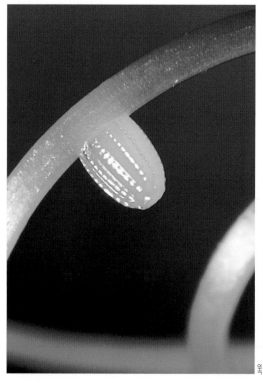

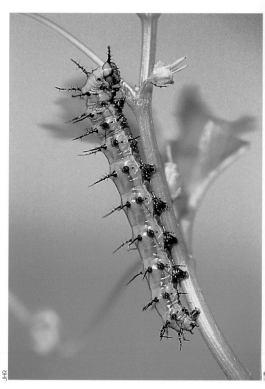

△ The Gulf Fritillary's egg is deposited on a tendril of the caterpillar's food plant, the passionflower vine. Each egg is strikingly sculpted with ribs.

△ A newly hatched Gulf Fritillary caterpillar next to a Gulf Fritillary egg. Note the silken thread spun by the larva to help it stick to the leaf.

△ The last-stage of a Gulf Fritillary caterpillar feeding on its passionflower host. Occasionally, larval spines are bent or broken by encounters with predators or falls.

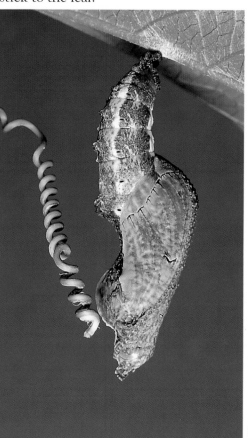

△ When a Gulf Fritillary caterpillar has finished feeding, it makes a silk pad on a stem, attaches its rear end to it, and hangs head down in a "J" position as it prepares to pupate. Note the head area swollen with fluid; soon the skin will split and roll back. Most Gulf Fritillary caterpillars roam away from their passionvine foodplants before pupating to avoid predators which may have learned to look for them on this plant.

△ The pupa of the Gulf Fritillary is seen here next to a spiralled tendril on its food plant, the passionflower vine. Butterflies usually remain in their pupa between seven days and several months, although some species can remain for years. When the butterfly is ready to emerge from its pupa, it produces a chemical which softens the material between the plates of the pupa. The bottom plate will then open like a trapdoor.

△ About ten days after it forms a pupa, the new, adult Gulf Fritillary butterfly splits its pupal shell and emerges. While hanging from its pupal shell, it pumps its wing veins full of fluid to expand its tiny, crumpled wings, and then waits for its wings to dry before taking its first flight. At this stage, the adult is very vulnerable to predation.

BUTTERFLY WINGS AND COLORS

To qualify for membership in the order Lepidoptera (butterflies and moths), an insect must have scale-covered wings. A butterfly or moth wing is a transparent membrane made of a material similar to human fingernails. This membrane is covered by a thin layer of wing-scales which are actually modified, flattened hairs. These scales stiffen and protect the wing somewhat, but the scales are very fragile and can be easily rubbed off, forming a fine dust. The dusty nature of the scales is something like milled flour. It is for this reason that certain moths are called dusty millers.

Although the wings of butterflies and some moths seem to be decked out in a rainbow of colors, it is very rare for any single butterfly or moth to have more than five distinct colors. Each wing scale is a single color. The seemingly wide variation of color is the result of varying intensity of a single color within each scale, the overlapping of two or more scales, and the reflection of light off the scales.

There are two types of colors in butterflies. Pigmented colors are chemical compounds whch are stored in the wing membranes and scales. These pigments may come from organic dyes in the host plant upon which the caterpillar feeds or may be manufactured by the caterpillar itself.

Most shades of red, orange, yellow and ivory are pigmented colors. Greens are from the chlorophyll in plants. Blacks, grays, tans, browns, brown-reds, and some yellow are melanins. Pigmented colors sometimes fade a bit after the death of a butterfly.

Structural colors are caused by the reflection of light off the scales. The metallic blues, greens, golds, and silvers seen in some butterflies are structural colors. These iridescent colors are created in the same manner as the rainbow of colors seen in a puddle of oil. Small ridges on the scale act like prisms, and by a process called diffraction, break white light into a variety of colors. Structual color remains strong after the death of a butterfly. Most butterflies and moths have both structural and pigment colors.

White occurs in butterfly wings when bubbles of air trapped within wing scales bounce back all the color wavelengths.

The often photographed morpho butterflies from Central and South America, prominently displayed at Butterfly World and Cypress Gardens, provide outstanding examples of structural color.

△ An extreme close-up of the wing of a Gulf Fritillary butterfly shows the detail of the scales. The light-colored scales are transparent, but the wing is not. The white-silvery color results from the refraction of light passing through the scales. The other scales in this view contain various pigments of brown and yellow-tan that make up part of the wing pattern.

△ The adult butterfly eye has many facets. This photo also shows the coiled feeding tube.

▷ This caterpillar's eyes are seen as tiny sparkles within the dark patches on each side of the its head. The orange-colored projections from the top of the head are odor weapons called an osmeteria.

THE BUTTERFLY EYE

This close-up of a newly emerged Gulf Fritillary butterfly shows in remarkable detail the large compound eye located on each side of the head and the coiled proboscis. Butterflies can perceive the widest range of colors in the animal kingdom, from ultraviolet to the red end of the color spectrum. Their compound eyes are made of individual facets which allow them to see an object as a mosaic of individual pieces. Each facet sees a portion of the total picture. The effect is comparable to the pixels or dots that make up a picture on a computer screen or television set. Some butterfly eyes have as many as 17,000 facets. The more facets, the finer the detail. However, the vision of insects may not be as sharp as that of humans. Humans have several million sensors in their eyes seemingly capable of producing much sharper images. But insects such as butterflies enjoy a much wider view. Some are capable of 360-degree vision. In addition, they are better at viewing moving images, an ability which enables them to perceive objects clearly during their erratic flight. Caterpillars have two sets of six simple eyes arranged in oval-shaped clusters, one on each side of the head. These rudimentary eyes may only perceive light and dark. Most caterpillars can see no further than a few inches. These eyes are actually enlarged ommatidia, the facets of which combine to make up the adult eye.

Brush-footed Butterflies

Family: Nymphalidae
Subfamily: True Nymphalinae

Phaon Crescent

In Greek mythology, Phaon was an old man who ferried the goddess of love, Aphrodite, to her destination. In return for his services, she gave him youth and beauty.

The Phaon Crescent can be distinguished from the Pearl Crescent by the pale cream band across the middle area of its front wings. This band is clearly evident on both sides of the wings. Its favorite habitats are roadsides and open fields that have been grazed or otherwise chopped.

Phyciodes phaon. Range: all of the Florida peninsula. Maximum wingspread: 1.3-1.5 inches. Months seen: March to November in northern Florida, every month to the south. Caterpillar food: lippia.

▷ This female Phaon Crescent has just emerged from its pupa. The Phaon Crescent is found in fields near its host plant, lippia, a low-growing ground cover.

Pearl Crescent

This very common crescent species has bright orange males and somewhat darker females; both sexes lack any trace of the pale cream band seen in the Phaon Crescent. It is one of Florida's most common and widespread butterflies and one of the first butterflies seen each spring on weedy lawns in urban areas.

Pearl Crescent caterpillars can be easily reared on aster plants, and since asters produce very attractive flowers, they are frequently planted in butterfly gardens to attract this species and establish it as a breeding resident in a yard.

Phyciodes tharos. Range: entire state of Florida. Maximum wingspread: 1.2-1.7 inches. Months seen: all but the winter months. Caterpillar food: asters.

◁ This Pearl Crescent has stopped for a moment on a tickseed flower (*Coreopsis*). The common name, Crescent, comes from the tiny, crescent-shaped marks along the edge of the hindwings.

WHY BUTTERFLIES BOUNCE AROUND AS THEY FLY

Compare a butterfly to a bee or a beetle, and it is obvious that the butterflies have made an absurdly big investment in disproportionately large wings. Who designed these butterflies, anyhow? Aside from the waste of materials in such an excessive wing area, their huge wings prevent butterflies from creeping into small holes for protection against enemies or weather, and they make flying butterflies conspicuous to every predator. Aircraft designs which match a gigantic wing with a small fusilage are not stable. Witness the "Flying Wing" aircraft built by Northrop some years ago. It didn't have enough equilibrium to fly safely until powerful computers had been invented to take over the controls, allowing it to reappear in a new form, the Stealth Bomber. But instability is not always bad; it may be the secret defense of butterflies. Butterflies are not the fastest fliers among the insects, but for unpredictable flips and erratic changes in direction, they are in a league of their own. Their huge wings allow them to fly rather slowly, and even glide, so they can drop in a sudden stall, then quickly pull up, or make a sudden upward hop. No predatory insect or bird flies quite like this, which makes it difficult for flying hunters to match their flight path to that of a butterfly. Think of the familiar upward spiral of a pair of butterflies, with its irregular, directional twitches and virtuoso near-misses. What other flying creature can barnstorm so brilliantly?

MD

Tawny Emperor

Populations of this large butterfly are rather isolated in Florida. They are always found in dense woods near hackberry trees, because their caterpillars feed on these trees. The males are very territorial and will defend their perches from other males. The caterpillars are yellowish-green with a long, narrow, dark green or blue stripe on top. The genus name, *Asterocampa*, means "starred caterpillar," a reference to the markings on its head.

Asterocampa clyton. Range in Florida: northern and central Florida. Maximum wingspread: 2-2.8 inches. Months seen: March to November. Generations per year: two. Caterpillar food: leaves of hackberry trees.

△ The Tawny Emperor is aptly named for the golden brown color of its upperside. Its mottled, underside allows this woodland creature to hide its brighter colors when it alights on bark and folds its wings.

▽ After the eggs of the Tawny Emperor hatch, the tiny larvae feed together. They remain together and do not disperse until the later larval stages.

△ The Tawny Emperor lays its eggs in neat rows on leaves of its caterpillar's food plant, the hackberry tree.

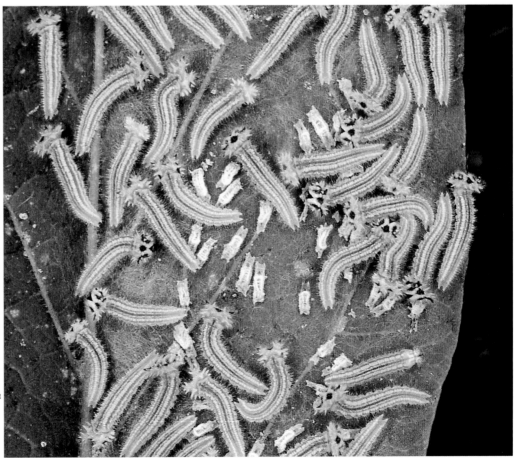

Brush-footed Butterflies

Family: Nymphalidae
Subfamily: True Nymphalinae

Virginia Lady

The Virginia Lady, sometimes called the American Painted Lady, occurs throughout much of North America. It lays eggs on cudweed (*Gnaphalium*), and the yellow-and-black-banded caterpillars that emerge make a little nest of silk at the top of the plant. They use the nest for resting during the day.

Adults are easily distinguished from the Painted Lady butterfly by the two very large eyespots on the underside of the hindwings. In addition, the Virginia Lady is more reddish on the underside of its front wings than the Painted Lady.

Vanessa virginiensis. Range in Florida: entire state; sporadic in South Florida and the Keys. When seen: March to December, but more common in the fall. Maximum wingspread: 2 inches. Months seen: every month. Caterpillar food: cudweeds.

△ The Virginia Lady caterpillar feeds on cudweed. It makes a nest for resting.

△ A Virginia Lady butterfly showing the pattern on the upperside of its wings and the enlarged eye-spots on the hindwings that distinguish it from the Painted Lady. The notch in the outer edge of the forewing (see arrow) that is typical of this genus .

▽ The Virginia Lady butterfly has an intricate pattern on its underside which resembles a spiderweb or a delicate tapestry. Note the large eyespots at the rear of the hind wing. The Virginia Lady usually holds its wings closed when feeding.

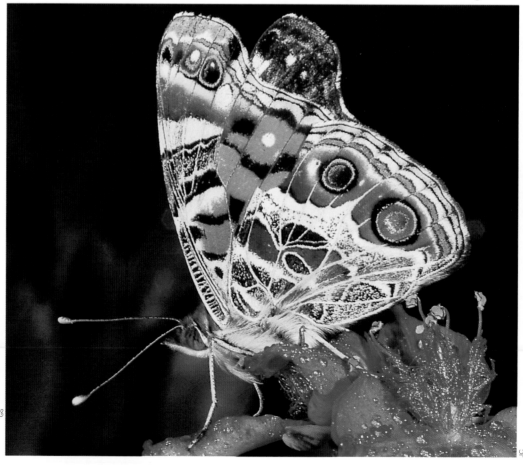

Painted Lady Butterfly

The Painted Lady has one of the greatest ranges of any butterfly. Its distribution is almost worldwide. For this reason, it is sometimes called the Cosmopolitan Butterfly. The Painted Lady is also among the most migratory of all butterflies. Millions of Painted Ladies fly north into Europe each spring from their North African desert breeding grounds.

Most Painted Ladies found in North America leave Mexico in the springtime and spend a generation or two in the southwestern deserts of the United States feeding on spring flowers. They then continue north as far as Canada, starting south again in the fall to return to the Tropics. At that time, fair numbers can be seen migrating south through Florida. Painted Ladies are more commonly seen in Texas than in Florida. The migrants which appear in Florida are most frequently seen in the Keys. The species is occasionally a seasonal resident of Florida in the Lower Keys, where the caterpillars feed on thistles that grow in the pinelands (it is sometimes known as the Thistle Butterfly).

Vanessa cardui. Range in Florida: spotted throughout the state, especially during migration in the fall, but mostly found in the Keys. Maximum wingspread: 2 inches. Caterpillar food: thistles.

△ Note the small eyespots on the undersides of the wings. This is the main difference between the Painted Lady and the Virginia Lady. Compare the large eyespots of the Virginia Lady in the photo at the bottom of the previous page.

△ The above photo of a female Painted Lady reveals a simple way to distinguish this species from the Virginia Lady when the wings are open. Notice that the Virginia Lady at the top of the opposite page has one white spot in the middle of a patch of orange on each forewing. The Painted Lady has white spots on its forewings, but none of these spots appears against an orange background.

Brush-footed Butterflies

Family: Nymphalidae
Subfamily: True Nymphalinae

Common Buckeye

Most Buckeye species live in the tropics, but the Common Buckeye resides across much of the southern United States and flies north each summer. This species cannot survive freezing temperatures in any stage, so it cannot reside year-round in the north. In Florida, Buckeyes prefer open fields and sand dune habitats, where adults can frequently be seen sunning themselves during the morning and midday hours.

The Common Buckeye caterpillar has pink and reddish-brown stripes and spines which are harmless to humans. Pink false foxglove is one of its many larval foods.

Junonia coenia. Range in Florida: entire state. When seen: all year, but more common during the summer. Maximum wingspread: 1.6-2.8 inches. Caterpillar food: members of the snapdragon family and a number of plantains.

△ The Common Buckeye is a familiar sight on Florida lawns and fields during spring and summer. It migrates north in the spring and south in the fall.

Goatweed Leafwing

The Goatweed Leafwing, also called the Goatweed Emperor, is one of two leafwing species in Florida. It is reddish-orange on its upperside and the color of dead leaves on its underside.

It gets the first part of its common name from the fact that one of its chief food plants is goatweed, a plant found in scattered, second-growth areas and suburban fields. The second part of its name is due to the fact that leafwing butterflies resemble

dead leaves when their wings are folded. Thus, they are superbly camouflaged when resting on the ground under trees which is covered with leaf litter. Their tails even resemble leaf stems.

Goatweed Leafwings prefer open, deciduous woods and scrubby habitats, especially along streams and open fields. The other Florida leafwing species, the Florida Leafwing, occurs only in South Florida and the Keys.

Anaea andria. Range in Florida: northern to north-central Florida. Maximum wingspread: 2.5-3.25 inches. Caterpillar food: croton or goatweed.

34

White Peacock

This mostly white butterfly has an attractive overlying pattern of wavy brown lines and bands, together with several eyespots and orange margins. It can be seen all year in south Florida and moves up into central and northeastern Florida each summer. It prefers weedy fields, either dry or moist, and uses a variety of food plants for its larvae, including lippia and water hyssop. The larvae are dark brown to black, with black spines and a black head with two long, club-like projections.

Anartia jatrophae. Range: South Florida as a breeding resident; Central and Northeastern Florida as a temporary colonist. Maximum wingspread: 2.3-2.8 inches. When seen: all year in south Florida. Caterpillar food: blechum, lippia and ruellia.

△ The caterpillar of the White Peacock butterfly, here seen feeding on ruellia, is black and spiny. Adults fly close to the ground and often perch on vegetation or visit flowers.

△ The upperside of the White Peacock butterfly is pearly white with delicate, wavy lines of brown and orange.

△ The White Peacock is a common butterfly in South Florida. It loves to visit flowers and usually opens its wings while basking in the sun or feeding.

Brush-footed Butterflies

Family: Nymphalidae
Subfamily: True Nymphalinae

Question Mark

Notice the irregular shape of the outline of the wings which is common to the members of this genus, *Polygonia*. This Latin name means "many angles." These butterflies are commonly called Anglewings. Another important feature is the camouflage coloration on the underside of the wings which helps the butterfly blend with bark. The jagged edge of the wings also helps this butterfly blend with its surroundings. The upperside may be bright, but when the butterfly lands and folds its wings, it can easily disappear from view.

The Question Mark feeds on rotting fruit and oozing tree sap. It is known for its habit of getting drunk when feeding on fermented fruit. It is then reluctant to fly and may stagger when walking.

Polygonia interrogationis. Range: North Florida. Maximum wingspread: 2.5-3 inches. Caterpillar food: stinging nettles and leaves of trees such as hackberry.

HOW CATERPILLARS MOVE

Caterpillars have three pairs of true legs, followed by as many as five pairs of "pro-legs" which function the same as the true legs. The true legs later develop into the legs of the adult butterfly, while the pro-legs are lost during metamorphosis.

Caterpillars are well designed for movement on the plants they eat. Their feet are capable of wrapping around and grasping the branches and stems. To move forward, the caterpillar lifts one pair of legs and slides them forward immediately followed by the pair of legs in front. This produces a wave-like motion.

Some caterpillars, such as those of the geometrid moths, do not have as many pro-legs and move by arching their body. These caterpillars are called loopers or inchworms.

△ The underside of a Question Mark's wing showing the famous "?" marking which gives this butterfly its name and also distinguishes it from a similar species called the Comma, whose underwing marking resembles a comma, or a question mark without the dot.

Red-spotted Purple

The Red-spotted Purple is a familiar sight in the woodlands of northern Florida, where it cruises along open lanes and alights in patches of sunlight. The males are somewhat territorial and may defend clearings and food sources such as rotting fruits and animal dung. This butterfly has an iridescent purple sheen on both sides of its wings. Because of its large size and dark color, a butterfly-watcher might mistake it for one of the swallowtails at first glance. In fact, it is a mimic of the foul-tasting Pipevine Swallowtail.

Limenitis arthemis astyanax. Range in Florida: Northern to Central Florida. Maximum wingspread: 3-4 inches. Months seen: spring to late fall. Caterpillar food: wild cherry.

Question Mark

Red-spotted Purple

BUTTERFLY EGGS

The eggs of butterflies and moths are wondrously intricate objects. The outer shell is frequently colorful. It may be sculptured with ribs and ridges; pitted, or smooth as a billiard ball. The egg can be flattened like a wrinkled turban (hairstreaks) barrel-shaped (many nymphalids), or staked like a string of pearls (Question Mark). At the egg's top are four holes through which the male's sperm cells swim to fertilize the egg.

Brush-footed Butterflies

Family: Nymphalidae
Subfamily: True Nymphalinae

Malachite

The Malachite butterfly (pronounced mal-a-kite) can be easily recognized by its large green wings. Its name comes from the mineral malachite, which is brilliant green.

This beautiful tropical species established itself in Florida only recently, but could lay claim to being Florida's most beautiful butterfly. Prior to 1965, only a few specimens were seen in the state. These were most likely strays from Cuba. But now, probably due to the natural dispersal of Malachites from Mexico or the Caribbean islands, they are abundant in places where food is available.

The Malachite has a slow, floating flight but can fly rapidly when disturbed. It is usually seen as it flies along the edges of weedy fields and woods.

The spectacular green color of the Malachite fades a bit a few days after it emerges from its pupa. The bright markings are also less vivid on older butterflies and fade quickly on dead specimens.

Note the short "tail" on each hind wing of the Malachite which is similar to that of the swallowtails, although the Malachite is not related. A number of butterflies other than swallowtails have this feature, including hairstreaks and leafwings.

For other views of this beautiful butterfly, see the photo on the front cover.

Siproeta stelenes. Range in Florida: southern Florida, including the Keys. Maximum wingspread: 3.3-4 inches. Months seen: all year. Caterpillar food: blechum, ruellia, plantago.

Red Admiral

The name Admiral probably refers to the uniform of a navy officer. The first admiral butterflies to be named were from England. These species had blue or black background colors with white spots which followed the colors of British naval uniforms of the period. However, some references insist that this butterfly's name is actually a corruption of the word "admirable." This explanation is less likely.

Along with the Painted Lady, the Red Admiral is one of the most widespread butterflies in the world. It is found across the entire northern hemisphere, from Europe to Asia to North America.

Because adult males often take territorial perches on sun-spotted driveways and other locations in the late afternoon, reappearing for many days in a row at exactly the same time and place, this butterfly has become familiar to many homeowners.

Red Admiral caterpillars feed on nettles in wet places, where they construct silken nests in leaves. The adults are frequently found near streams and marshes or in moist city parks and fields.

Vanessa atalanta. Range: entire state of Florida. Maximum wingspread: 2.5-3 inches. Months seen: All year. Caterpillar food: nettles.

▷ The mottled underside of the Red Admiral helps to conceal it, in contrast to its vivid, red-striped, black upperside.

▽ The orange-red markings on the uppersides of the front and hind wings appear to merge together, forming almost a complete circle.

Brush-footed Butterflies

Family: Nymphalidae
Subfamily: True Nymphalinae

Ruddy Daggerwing

Adult daggerwings have a long, thin "dagger" projecting like a tail from the rear edge of the hindwing. The Ruddy Daggerwing can be found in southern Florida wherever strangler figs grow. The caterpillars feed on the leaves of strangler figs and may be distasteful to birds, but scientists have not yet verified this. Ruddy Daggerwings like to visit moist places on river banks and roadside mud puddles, as well as rotting fruits and flowers.

Marpesia petreus. Range: southern to central Florida. Maximum wingspread: 3-3.8 inches. Months seen: all year. Caterpillar food: fig trees, strangler figs.

△ The daggerwing caterpillar is vividly colored and grotesque with its various appendages. These pattern elements help break up its outline, making it less conspicuous to a searching predator.

▽ The Ruddy Daggerwing, a vivid, orange butterfly with thin black stripes, occurs in abundance at times in the Miami area , the Florida Keys, and the Big Cypress Swamp.

Florida Viceroy

The Florida Viceroy butterfly is a rich brown color in the southern part of Florida, where it mimics the Queen, and red-orange in the northern counties, where it mimics the Monarch. It prefers swamps and moist areas along streams and lake edges, where willow trees prosper in the moist soils.

Limenitis archippus floridensis. Range in Florida: entire state. Maximum wingspread: 3.3 inches. Months seen: all year. Caterpillar food: willows.

△ The underside of a Viceroy Butterfly, seen as it feeds on ixora flowers.

△ The Viceroy caterpillar has a white blotch on top and white sides and looks like a bird dropping (the chrysalis also has the same appearance). The caterpillar is well camouflaged on its willow food plants.

Viceroy and Red-spotted Purple caterpillars are nearly identical in appearance, with the horns shorter in the Viceroy. The caterpillar of the Giant Swallowtail also resembles a bird dropping.

NOT JUST A MIMIC OF BAD TASTE, BUT REALLY TASTES BAD

Because the Viceroy caterpillar feeds on willow, a plant which was thought to be harmless, it was widely assumed at one time by biologists that the Viceroy butterfly was an edible mimic of the bad-tasting Monarch and Queen butterflies. However, recent studies show that the caterpillar takes chemicals from the willow leaves such as salicylic acid (the bitter-tasting ingredient in aspirin) that, while not poisonous, make it unacceptable to lizards and birds. Thus, the Viceroy is not just faking bad taste to avoid predators; it really tastes bad. Its coloration, which is similar to that of the Queen and Monarch, thus helps reinforce the warning to predators, "Leave us alone. You won't like us."

Satyrs & Wood Nymphs

Family: Satyridae

In classical mythology, satyrs were half-man, half-goat creatures, and nymphs, their female counterparts, were beautiful maidens. Both had a reputed tendency to go dancing naked through the woods. Butterflies of the family satyridae are known for their erratic, bobbing, bouncing flight through wooded areas, a movement which could be described as dancing. This may be the origin of their names.

The camouflage colors on the undersides of their wings help them to hide when they land on grasses or tree trunks. They also hide by tilting their wings to avoid casting a shadow.

Satyrs are known for the eyespot patterns on the underside of their wings which may distract predators from the head of the butterfly (when the butterfly is at rest) in a manner similar to the tail-like wing extensions of the swallowtails and hairstreaks. They also have very small forelegs, like those of the brush-footed butterflies.

Satyr caterpillars are usually green with stripes. They have forked tails and feed on grass. It is not yet known why their tails are forked.

Carolina Satyr (Above)

This small, plain butterfly inhabits shady grassy areas and is often the most abundant butterfly in the Florida woods. Note the eyespots along the hind wing.

The adults flock to rotting fruit to sip the juices rather than seeking nectar from flowers. They pose no danger to fruit crops because they cannot open fruit. They only feed on fruit that is rotting, has fallen, or is already damaged by other insects.

This butterfly has also been known as the Hermes Satyr. Under this name, the butterfly's range extends along the east coast of the US to as far south as Argentina, one of the largest geographic distributions of any butterfly. However, it now appears that the Hermes Satyr is actually a complex composed of a number of species.

Hermeuptychia sosybius. Range in Florida: entire state. Months seen: all year. Maximum wingspan: 1-1.2 inches. Caterpillar food: grasses.

Little Wood Satyr (Left)

This satyr has a pair of extremely prominent eyespots along the edge of each wing. It frequents woody areas and forest edges.

Adults normally feed on tree sap flows and aphid honeydew but occasionally visit flowers of milkweed and sweet clover.

Megisto cymela. Range in Florida: North Florida. Months seen: April-June primarily. Maximum wingspan: 1-1.2 inches. Caterpillar food: grasses.

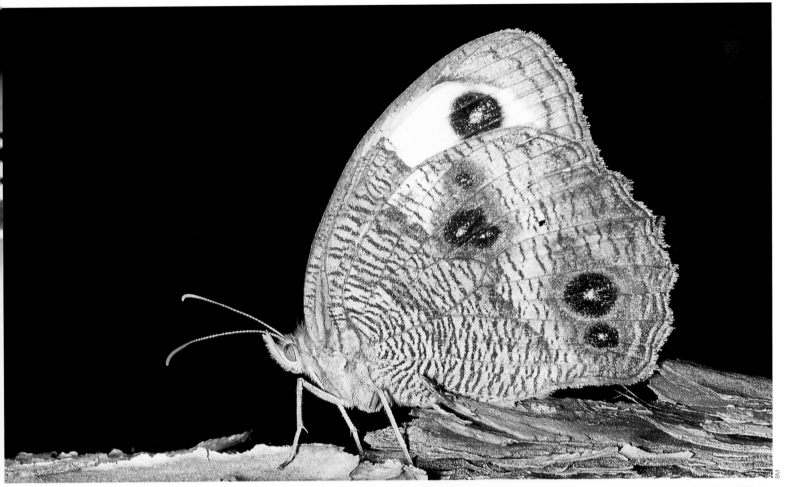

Pearly-eyed Wood Nymph

The Pearly-eyed Wood Nymph is a large, brown butterfly with two large, yellow-rimmed eyespots on each front wing. It is found in small numbers in grassy areas in the pine forests of North Florida. Its characteristic bouncing flight makes it immediately distinguishable in summer. This wood nymph visits flowers for nectar (unlike most other wood nymphs which feed on fruit). The caterpillars feed on grass. Although they hatch from eggs in early fall, they don't begin to feed, surprisingly, until the following spring. They remain in the first larval stage through the winter. Many races of this butterfly are found across the United States, and their wing colors are quite variable, even within Florida.

Cercyonis pegala. Range in Florida: the Panhandle and northern Florida, down to Central Florida along the Atlantic coast. Maximum wingspread: 2.5-3 inches. Months seen: June to September. Generations per year: one. Caterpillar food: grasses.

THE VALUE OF EYESPOTS

Most satyrs and wood nymphs have eyespots on the undersides of their wings. When camouflage fails, these eyespots attract the strikes of predators such as birds. The butterfly may escape with only a small piece of wing missing. It can afford to lose an eyespot, whereas the loss of its head would be fatal. Some biologists think that eyespots may be frightening to small birds or lizards and make them think twice about attacking.

Georgia Satyr

This beautiful little wood nymph has soft brown wings with a row of long eyespots and red-orange lines on the underside of each hindwing. The adults are found in sandy pinewood areas, where they feed on rotting fruit, but they are never seen at flowers. The caterpillar is yellowish-green with yellow stripes, and it feeds on sedges.

Neonympha aurelata. Range in Florida: entire state. Maximum wingspread: 1.75 inches. Months seen: most of the year. Caterpillar food: sedges.

Milkweed Butterflies

Family: Danaidae

Milkweed butterflies are sometimes called "royalty butterflies" because their family (Danaidae) was named after the daughters of Danaus, the ruler of Argos. Danaus married his daughters to their cousins but made them slaughter their husbands on their wedding night.

Male milkweed butterflies have scent scales on their wings and structures on their abdomens called "hair pencils" which also secrete scent. The scent is used during courtship. During copulation, the male and female remain attached for about 30 to 60 minutes (the average length of time for most species).

The color pattern of milkweed butterflies is easy to spot because of the black margin around the edge of the wings with bright color inside. The caterpillars of milkweed butterflies feed mostly on milkweed plants. They accumulate toxins from these plants which remain in the bodies of the pupae and adults and make them highly distasteful to some predators.

There are only three butterflies of the genus *Danaus* in the United States: the Monarch, Queen, and Soldier.

Monarchs and Queens have a distinctive flight pattern which consists of vigorous flapping followed by a long glide. It is this ability to soar and glide which helps the Monarch cover great distances during its annual migrations.

▷ A male Monarch feeding on a milkweed flower. The female will later lay her eggs on the leaves of this plant.

Monarch

The Monarch, probably the most familiar of all U.S. butterflies, may soon be proclaimed the national insect, a designation for which it has been nominated. It is bright orange, with a white-spotted black border and black-outlined veins. The male has a black scent patch in the middle of each hindwing.

The caterpillar, dramatically ringed with yellow, black, and white on each segment, has a pair of black fleshy tubercles at each end. The larvae feed on perhaps 100 different species of milkweeds throughout their range in North America.

During the warm part of the year, this species goes through as many as six broods in southern Florida, where it may remain resident year-round. In the rest of the state, however, and in most of the continent, the species is highly migratory.

Danaus plexippus. Range in Florida: entire state. Maximum wingspread: 4.9 inches. Months seen: March to September, except southernmost Florida, where they may be seen all year. Caterpillar food: milkweed.

△ The black spot on each hindwing of the male Monarch butterfly is a cluster of scent scales. The scent is used in courtship.

MIMICRY CIRCLES: MONARCH, QUEEN, AND VICEROY

There are two important kinds of mimicry found in butterflies. Batesian Mimicry refers to a kind of mimicry where only one species, the model, is poisonous or otherwise unpleasant to predators; it is usually marked with bright warning colors. Harmless species in the same environment may come to resemble the model species through genetic mutation and natural selection. These harmless mimics gain protection by their resemblance to the model insect, increasing the chance that they will survive. In this way, a defenseless flower fly that has evolved to resemble a stinging bee is afforded some degree of protection by that resemblance. This type of mimicry is termed Batesian mimicry in honor of its discoverer, Henry Walter Bates, an English naturalist who first observed it among butterflies on the Amazon River in the 19th century.

Another kind of mimicry is Mullerian mimicry, discovered by Fritz Muller, also along the Amazon, a few years after Bates' work. In Mullerian mimicry, a number of noxious species all display the same color pattern, but in this case, they are not faking it. They all really do taste bad. Predators that have a bad experience with one member of the group remember the pattern when they encounter another, thus reinforcing the protection for all members of the group.

In Florida, the Monarch, Viceroy, and Queen grouping is such a complex. All three species are distasteful. The Monarch and Queen caterpillars feed on milkweeds, and incorporate poisonous compounds from the plants into their skins. The Viceroy acquires its bad taste from leaves of the willow tree, the source of salicylic acid, a major ingredient of aspirin.

△ Monarch and Queen Butterflies on milkweed, showing the similarity on the underside of their wings. The Queen is the darker butterfly on the left.

△ The Viceroy is an excellent mimic of the Queen Butterfly in Florida and rather closely resembles the Monarch as well. The curving black line across its hindwings distinguishes the Viceroy from both the Queen and the Monarch.

△ A male Monarch butterfly. Note the scent pouches in the center of the hindwings.

◁ A male Queen butterfly. Note the scent pouches in the middle portion of the hindwings.

45

Milkweed Butterflies

Family: Danaidae

MONARCH MIGRATION

Every year, most Monarch butterflies undertake a truly remarkable migration. In the fall, starting in early September, hundreds of millions of Monarchs fly south from the eastern part of the United States to Mexico. They either fly through peninsular Florida and then across the Gulf or follow the panhandle west and go south through Texas. In Florida, these Monarchs may stop at places such as the St. Marks National Wildlife Refuge or Sanibel Island for a few days of rest. Some of those that cross the Gulf stop briefly to rest on oil drilling platforms. They ultimately make their way to several spots in the mountains of the state of Michoacan, about 100 miles west of Mexico City. There, by mid-November, they cover the branches of fir trees in these mountain refuges nearly 11,000 feet above sea level.

The Monarchs spend the winter in colonies which may contain 100 million or more butterflies in an area no larger than 10 to 20 acres. As many as a dozen or more of these colonies form each winter, meaning that perhaps a billion or more North American Monarchs spend the winter in this extraordinarily restricted area.

From November to mid-March, the butterflies cling to the trees, surviving on their stored fat, with occasional visits to streams and other moist places for water. Severe freezes can kill large numbers of Monarchs on these roosts, but temperatures normally hover above freezing. The cool winter temperatures cause the butterflies' metabolic rate to drop. Their slower metabolism is what enables them to survive for so many months without food.

Several species of birds, including orioles and grosbeaks, have learned that they can feed upon certain edible parts of the Monarch—parts that are not protected by the poisons the butterflies absorb from their larval food plants—but hundreds of millions of butterflies nevertheless survive until spring.

In mid-March, the survivors become active. They know, probably from the lengthening days, that it is time to fly north. They mate at the site and start north, stopping near the Mexican border or in the southern United States to mate again, perhaps, and lay their eggs. At this point, the butterflies heading north from Mexico die. In April or May, their offspring fly further north to the central United States, lay their eggs and die. Not until the next generation do Monarchs once more reach the northernmost states and south-

ern Canada. Around the first of September, the adults turn south again to begin the long journey back to that remote spot in central Mexico.

This amazing migratory journey is even more remarkable when one considers that the Monarchs flying south in the fall have never made the journey before. They are the grandchildren or great-grandchildren of butterflies that made the very same trip the previous year. When they leave their breeding places in eastern North America to head for Mexico, they do not know any landmarks. But somehow, they make a bee-line (or butterfly-line, in this case) toward the proper site, where many will survive the winter.

This journey of up to 2,000 miles is driven by instinct, and how the monarchs find their way is still very much a mystery. The butterflies seem to be guided by celestial navigation in their flight, perhaps utilizing the orientation of the sun. As they reach the mountains where they will spend the winter, it is believed that they are guided by magnetic fields in the area. Each Monarch has tiny particles of magnetite in the expanded bases of its wing veins. These magnetic particles may act as tiny compasses and point the butterflies toward large

△ Monarch butterflies assembling on shrubs and trees at St. Mark's National Wildlife Refuge in North Florida. These butterflies are getting ready to cross the Gulf to their winter home in Mexico.

◁ A researcher at the refuge tags a Monarch on the forewing to study its flight patterns from the United States to Mexico. Remarkably, Monarchs have in this century extended their range to include such remote, cross-oceanic destinations as Europe, Hawaii, Australia, and New Zealand.

deposits of metallic ore in the vicinity of their winter colonies. What finally guides the migrating butterflies to the trees on which they will roost, the same trees their grandparents used the year before, may be the scent of billions of scales from the previous year's butterflies.

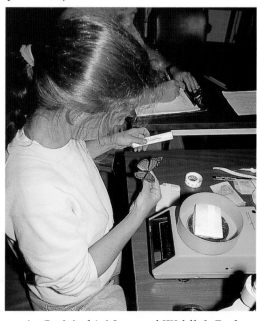

△ At St. Mark's National Wildlife Refuge in the Florida Panhandle, researchers determine the sex, wing length, and weight of a migrating Monarch butterfly.

△ The Monarchs' winter colonies in the state of Michoacan, Central Mexico, reach incredible densities. There may be 100 million Monarchs in a single colony in an area covering no more than 10 acres. The butterflies festoon the trees from the bottom of the trunks to the tops of the highest branches. Certain species of orioles and grosbeaks are unaffected by milkweed poisons and are attracted to these huge congregations. Their feasting is estimated to reduce Monarch populations by about ten percent, but the populations are large enough to easily absorb these losses.

◁ A sign in Michoacan, Mexico, near one of the Monarchs' winter colonies, reads, "Driver: Protect the Monarch butterfly. Slow down."

Milkweed Butterflies

Family: Danaidae

MONARCH LIFE CYCLE

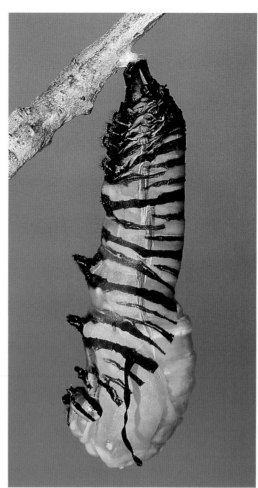

△ A Monarch butterfly larva, preparing to pupate, hangs in a J-shaped position from a pad of silk that it attached to the stem.

△ The last-stage Monarch caterpillar begins shedding its larval skin to reveal the new, soft chrysalis inside.

△ After the larval skin has been shed, the newly formed pupa of the Monarch has a soft, amorphous form before it hardens.

△ The newly hardened pupa of the Monarch butterfly glistens in the morning sun. Note the tiny gold dots scattered across a soft green background. It is easy to see why the butterfly pupa is called a chrysalis, a word meaning an "object of gold."

△ Near the end of the pupal stage, the developing adult butterfly can be seen through its pupal case.

△ About an hour or two before its emergence, the adult's legs and body parts show clearly through the transparent pupal skin.

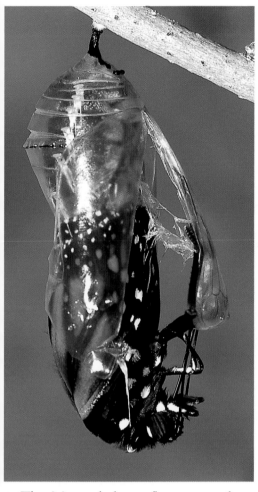  

△ The Monarch butterfly emerges from the pupa by first splitting the case along the length of its proboscis, near the head.

△ After the Monarch adult gets its legs out, it hangs vertically from the shell. Note the body swollen with fluid.

△ Now hanging freely from its pupal shell, the Monarch begins pumping fluid from its body into the veins of its soft wings.

△ The wings continue to expand from the pressure of the butterfly's body fluid coursing through its veins. The body shrinks to normal size.

△ After its wings are completely expanded, the adult allows them to dry as it hangs from the pupal skin. Within a couple of hours, the wings will be hard and capable of flight.

Milkweed Butterflies

Family: Danaidae

Queen

The Queen butterfly is a showy resident of Florida. It breeds on milkweed plants, along with its cousin, the Monarch. The Queen, however, tends to be a more poisonous butterfly in Florida than either the Monarch or the Viceroy, both of which mimic the Queen. The Queen caterpillar is a lot like that of the Monarch, with yellow, brown, and tannish-white rings on each segment.

Adult Queen butterflies prefer flying in open areas and along rivers. They stray as far north as Massachusetts.

The dark-colored scent scale pouches on the hindwings reveal that the adult in the top photo is a male.

Danaus gilippus. Range in Florida: entire state. Maximum wingspread: 3 7/8 inches. Months seen: every month. Caterpillar food: milkweed.

△ The underside of the Queen butterfly very closely resembles that of the Monarch. Both species are distasteful to predators and resemble each other for mutual protection. Scientists call this a Mullerian mimicry complex (see page 45).

◁ The pupa of the Queen butterfly is very similar to that of the Monarch. Note the similar gold spots on the thorax. (Compare the Monarch pupa on page 48.)

▷ The Queen caterpillar differs from the Monarch by having three pairs of thread-like tubercles on its body. The Monarch caterpillar has just two pairs, one pair at the head and the other at its tail.

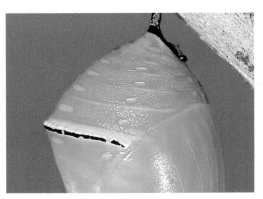

50

LEAF ROLLING

Some caterpillars have the ability to tie or roll a leaf into a tube to form a shelter which protects them from rain and wind and also helps to hide them from predators. A few of the most common techniques are shown on this page.

△ A Brazilian or Canna Skipper caterpillar rolls a leaf of canna, its food plant, by shortening a strand of silk that it attaches to either side of the leaf. The Brazilian Skipper caterpillar remains in the shelter while feeding. When it has devoured one section of the leaf, it moves to a new location and constructs a new shelter there before feeding again. The Spicebush Swallowtail caterpillar, on the other hand, uses its shelter only for resting and comes out to feed on the open leaves.

▷ The Spicebush Swallowtail caterpillar spins a web of silk that draws together the sides of a leaf and makes it into a tube. The front end of the caterpillar, with its fierce-looking, eye-like markings, is visible when the larva is at rest in the tube and appears threatening to potential enemies.

The Spicebush caterpillar has five stages of growth (instars). Although the last two resemble a snake, the first three resemble bird droppings. The countershading along the midbody line breaks up the body outline, making it look like anything but a caterpillar.

▽ The Bougainvillea Moth caterpillar uses a web of silk as a protective tent. The moth lives in this tent when not feeding in the open.

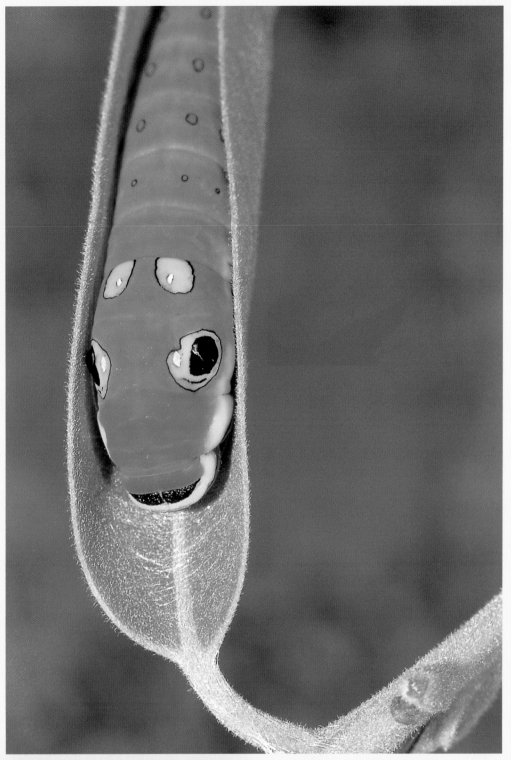

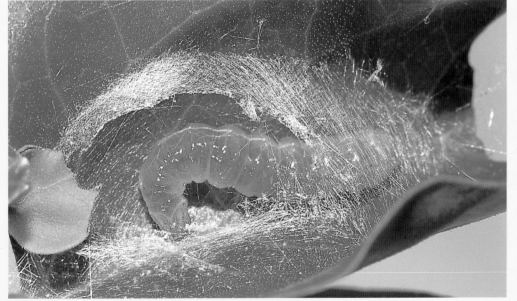

Butterflies and moths begin their adult lives with a supply of nutrients remaining from their earlier stage as caterpillars. This is enough to support some butterflies or moths throughout their remaining brief lives so that they do not need to feed at all. (The two giant skippers in Florida do not feed as adults. They utilize stored carbohydrates and fats from their larval stages.) In fact, some of the Saturnid moths even lack the mouth parts needed for feeding.

Some caterpillars, when feeding, avoid calling attention to themselves with piles of excrement by flinging each piece off the leaf or stem onto the ground, where it is less likely to be noticed by a predator.

Skippers

Family: Hesperiidae

Skippers are named for their quick, darting flight in which they seem to skip from one flower to another. They have thick, heavy, furry bodies and long, narrow wings. Like military fighter planes, they must fly fast to remain airborne. At rest, they assume a variety of postures. More characteristics of skippers include widely spaced antennae, the triangular shape of the wings and the fact that the eyes almost touch each other in the front of the face. Their antennae have tiny hooks at the tips of the knobs.

The family is divided into six subfamilies based on a number of esoteric features. There are many skipper species which are small and brownish, making identification sometimes rather difficult.

Although their colors are generally dull, there are some especially beautiful species in Florida, including the Mangrove Skipper, Brazilian Skipper, Long-tailed Skipper, and the Fiery Yellow Skipper.

Skipper caterpillars are usually smooth skinned and have big heads. Many can produce grating sounds by scraping their jaws across leaves.

Long-tailed Skipper

The Long-tailed Skipper can be readily recognized by the long tails on its hindwings and the iridescent blue flush on the upper surfaces of its wings. Adults frequently visit flowers of lantana and many composites, including Spanish needles (*Bidens*). The Long-tailed Skipper is especially abundant in the fall, when large numbers migrate into peninsular Florida from more northern points of the United States.

Urbanus proteus proteus. Range in Florida: peninsular Florida; more sporadic in the Florida Keys. When seen: all year. Maximum wingspread: 1.8-2.3 inches. Caterpillar food: beans and other legumes.

△ A Long-tailed Skipper with its wings open, warming itself in the morning sun.

△ The Long-tailed Skipper larva is also called the Bean Leaf Roller. Garden beans are often its host.

▷ This Long-tailed Skipper is feeding on the flowers of Spanish needles. It is a common migrant in Florida in the fall, when the populations of the northeastern United States fly south to the tropics.

Mangrove Skipper

The Mangrove Skipper is one of Flori-da's largest and most beautiful skippers. This male is feeding on pentas flowers.

Phocides pigmalion. Range in Florida: Keys and coastal areas of South Florida. Months seen: all year. Caterpillar food: the leaves of red mangrove trees.

▷ The female Mangrove Skipper is duller than its slightly iridescent male compan-ion (above). The female lays her eggs singly on red mangroves, and when the larvae hatch, they feed on the mangrove leaves.

Skippers are often mistaken for moths because of their stout, hairy bodies and short, pointed wings. Their heads are as wide as their bodies. They are sometimes classified as an intermediate form between true butterflies and true moths. Some scientists even classify them as a superfamily, equal in status to both butterflies and moths.

Tropical Checkered Skipper

The Tropical Checkered Skipper has a very distinctive pattern: black checks ar-ranged in bands on a white background. Males have numerous, long, bluish-white hairs on the uppersides of their wings. Fe-males are quite a bit darker than the males. The males fly low to the ground in weedy, disturbed sites patrolling for females. Both sexes can often be seen feeding at flowers. The larvae feed on young leaves of plants in the mallow or hibiscus family. The cater-pillar folds and ties leaves together to make a shelter in which it hides during much of the day.

Pyrgus oileus oileus. Range in Florida: peninsular Florida and the Florida Keys. Maximum wingspread: 1.2-1.5 inches. Months seen: every month. Caterpillar food: mallows.

Skippers

△ A close-up view of a Fiery Skipper butterfly shows the short, clubbed antennae typical of its family, Hesperiidae.

The Fiery Skipper gets its name from the bright golden-yellow color of the males. Females are mostly dark brown with golden-yellow spots above. Adults perch on low vegetation in weedy sites and visit garden flowers quite frequently.

△ The skipper's proboscis can reach deep into long flowers to sip nectar.

△ Note the "elbow" in the feeding tube which allows it to bend and gives butterflies great flexibility when reaching for nectar.

◁ The Whirl-about Skipper (*Polites vibex*) has a narrowish underside with a darkly outlined, pale central patch.

△▽▷ Many skippers are dull in color and relatively difficult to identify, such as the Florida Dusky Wing *Ephyriades brunnea floridensis* (above), the Delaware Skipper *Atrytone logan* (below), and the Sachem Skipper *Atalopedes campestris* (at right).

△ This mature caterpillar of the Zestos Skipper, *Epargyreus zestos zestos*, found in the Keys, shows the constricted neck which is characteristic of all skipper caterpillars.

YUCCA PLANT, YUCCA MOTH, AND YUCCA SKIPPER: AN AMAZING RELATIONSHIP

The attractive yucca plant which grows in pinelands and beach areas of Florida has an amazing relationship with a moth and a butterfly which serves each species well. The Yucca Skipper is one of two giant skipper species found in Florida. After mating, the female Yucca Skipper glues a single, large egg to the surface of a spiny yucca leaf. After hatching, the young larva eats the leaves, protected by a silk nest. As it grows older, it bores into a leaf and goes down the inside of the leaf into the stem, ending up inside one of the sucker roots underground. After completing its development inside the root, it breaks out of the root into the soil and creates a tunnel leading upwards to the surface. There it builds a emergence tower extending several inches above the ground and composed of camouflage materials. It then retreats into its tunnel and returns to the root, where it pupates. The Yucca Skipper pupa can move within its tunnel by wiggling. It is the only butterfly pupa that is capable of deliberate movement over any distance. It regulates its temperature during the winter by moving up the plant stem tunnel to catch the heat of the day and down beneath ground level at night for insulation from the cold. After the adult emerges from its pupa within the tunnel in March or April, it crawls out of the root and up the tunnel to the emergence tower. There it secretes an enzyme to dissolve the silken end. This allows the adult to hang from the tower while its wings inflate, and then fly away. The easiest way to find Yucca Skippers is to look for their eggs on yucca leaves or their larval tents on the ground nearby. The adults are very fast-flying and only live a few days, so they are rarely seen.

THE YUCCA MOTH

The adult Yucca Moth, Tegeticula yuccasella, is a totally different creature from the Yucca Skipper. It eats pollen and pollinates the yucca flower. It is night-flying, but may be seen during the day resting on yucca flowers. The female Yucca Moth uses a long, curved tentacle on the side of its mouth to collect pollen from the stamens of the yucca flower. It then flies to a different flower, where it inserts pollen and one egg into each chamber of the flower's ovary. This pollinates the flower and the resulting yucca seeds provide a food supply for the larvae when the eggs hatch. A single larva cannot eat all of the many seeds produced in each chamber, thus assuring that there will be new yucca plants to provide for Yucca Moths in the future. The Yucca Moth's amazing reproductive plan with its strict limit of one egg per chamber assures the survival of the yucca plant as well as the Yucca Moth.

CATERPILLAR WATCHING

Watching caterpillars is every bit as rewarding as watching butterflies. Caterpillars are soft sculptures, whose clever tucks and gussets are animated by an elaborate bed of criss-crossing muscles. Their movements have the grace of shifting fluids and are remarkably exact and deliberate. Early naturalists termed the larva the "imperfect form," and the adult, "the perfect form." This judgments was wrong. The idea that adults are attractive and interesting, while the young are disgusting and dull, is as absurd when applied to butterflies as it is when applied to humans.

Watching caterpillars has the added advantage that it can take place at leisure in a comfortable setting, since caterpillars perform well indoors in a small chamber. Raising caterpillars is usually easy, involving more common sense than technical expertise. Most caterpillars feed on a limited variety of plants, so it makes sense to provide the caterpillar with fresh leaves of the same type of plant on which it or its eggs were found.

When brought indoors, caterpillars are protected from a huge variety of natural enemies, especially birds and various wasps and flies that are dedicated caterpillar hunters. They are still subject, however, to bacterial and fungal diseases, so the container should be kept clean, with some ventilation.

Before pupating, a caterpillar may have a spurt of wanderlust, trying to distance itself from its food plant, whose gnawed leaves may attract the attention of predators. If a caterpillar does this, the remains of its plant should be removed from the jar. Most butterfly caterpillars need a twig or a piece of rough bark on which to hang the chrysalis, although some caterpillars can even hang from the side of a glass jar. Moth caterpillars often make a cocoon in curled dead leaves or burrow in loose earth or sand, both of which can be put in the bottom of the container as soon as the caterpillar loses interest in feeding.

For the beginning Florida caterpillar farmer, the two passionvine caterpillars, the Gulf Fritillary and the Zebra Longwing, are highly recommended. Sections of the native blue passionvine keep fresh for weeks if their stems are given fresh water. It is best to put the stems in a bottle with a narrow mouth so that the caterpillars will not fall in. The caterpillars often pupate on the vines, making a chrysalis that looks like a crumpled leaf. These species breed throughout the year, and emerge from the chrysalis promptly, in about a week, unlike some butterflies that remain in the chrysalis much longer (even until spring). The Zebra Longwing does not usually move far from where it has food plants and a shady retreat, so it is possible to augment the numbers of these butterflies in a backyard. However, the Gulf Fritillary, like most butterflies, often starts its adult life with a dispersal flight.

Raising butterflies intensifies understanding of the wonder of metamorphosis. There is no reason to believe that a caterpillar confined with its host plant is even aware of its captivity, and the release of native butterflies is unlikely to cause ecological problems. Caterpillar culture does not interfere with nature but draws nature closer to view.

THE REASON FOR METAMORPHOSIS

Most people know that butterflies come from caterpillars. But few ever really consider what is the purpose of this unusual life cycle. Why should nature bother to change a perfectly good caterpillar into a butterfly or a moth? Nature must have a good reason to create two creatures in the place of one, and there is a good reason: specialization. A highly specialized creature can do one task supremely well, better than a creature that is designed to perform several jobs.

The caterpillar is designed to eat and grow large. In fact, caterpillars have often been described as "eating machines." This is their only function, and their design is well suited to the task. They consist of a set of strong jaws connected to a digestive tube with an opening for waste. A caterpillar can eat twice its own weight in a day. It only stops feeding briefly to molt its skin.

On the other hand, adult butterflies and moths are designed to find a mate, reproduce and disperse. Some moths are so specialized for these tasks that the adults do not eat at all during their short lives. They simply fly, reproduce, and die. Special scents and receptors allow male and female butterflies or moths to find each other. Strong wings allow for dispersal of the eggs and the precise placement of the eggs on a food supply, so that the next generation of caterpillars has no need to travel.

THE MIRACLE OF METAMORPHOSIS

Butterflies, like other insects, have a skeleton surrounding the outside of their bodies to which the muscles are attached. This is called an exoskeleton. It is composed of hard plates connected by soft tissue and resembles a suit of armor. The hard material is called chitin and is somewhat like the material of human fingernails. One problem with this kind of skeleton is that it cannot grow and must be shed periodically to allow the caterpillar to grow. In animals with an internal skeleton, like humans, the skeleton can grow larger along with the rest of the body.

The process of shedding (molting) its external skeleton goes on through the entire life of a caterpillar. It may molt from four to nine times, depending on its species. Eventually, caterpillars undergo an elaborate extension of the molting process called metamorphosis. The caterpillar molts to a pupa and the pupa molts to become a butterfly, one of the most dramatic occurances in naure.

Metamorphosis has excited human observers for thousands of years, but only in the last few decades has the process been fully understood. Here is how it is accomplished. During each caterpillar stage, small changes occur which start the development of the wings, antennae, legs and other organs. Much of the growth of the new organs occurs within the 24-48 hours before the caterpillar molts to a pupa. When the skin of the caterpillar splits to reveal the pupal case underneath, it is possible to see the wings, legs, and even the feeding tube under the surface. During the pupal stage, the muscles and other remaining tissues of the former caterpillar change into a soup-like suspension of cells which reorganize themselves around various centers, such as the flight muscles, wings, etc. This finishes the transformation of a plant-eating, many-legged caterpillar into a nectar-sucking, six-legged, winged butterfly. Such a change requires that almost every body system, such as digestion, excretion, and respiration, be created anew.

When the pupa molts to reveal the adult butterfly, the new butterfly expands its folded wings by pumping blood through its hollow veins. It accomplishes this by swallowing air into the upper part of its digestive system, increasing its blood pressure as much as 15 times. The wings dry in an hour or two. The veins also dry out and become rigid supports for the wing membranes stretched between them.

The butterfly, now ready for flight, may vent a dark-colored fluid, often red in color, from the end of its abdomen, which makes it appear that it is bleeding. This fluid is actually composed of waste products that accumulated during the pupal stage, which the new butterfly now eliminates.

(See photos of the complete process on pages 28 and 48.)

BUTTERFLY PREDATORS

Butterflies are preyed upon at all stages of their lives. Ants eat their eggs, wheelbugs and toads eat the caterpillars, and pupae are eaten by wasp larvae. Adult butterflies are attacked by birds and a number of insects.

△ A praying mantis stalks a White Peacock.
▷ An ambush bug attacks a skipper.
▽ A wheel bug catches a caterpillar.

△ How can tiny bugs overcome much larger prey such as butterflies? This ambush bug uses its powerful hind legs to grip the flower while its front legs hold the butterfly. It uses its sharp beak to stab the butterfly repeatedly until it is subdued. Some bugs can even inject poison. The praying mantis uses its arms to immobilize a butterfly's wings as it begins to chew.

Swallowtails

△ A male Eastern Black Swallowtail sipping nectar on red flowers. The female's coloration is almost all blue-black and mimics that of the Pipevine Swallowtail, a species which many predators find distasteful.

Family: Papilionidae

Eastern Black Swallowtail

This attractive butterfly's Latin name comes from Polyxena, daughter of Priamos, King of Troy, from the *Iliad*, Homer's epic poem. Although this swallowtail is locally abundant in much of Florida, it is rare in the Keys where its larval food plants (members of the carrot family) are lacking. Males like to perch on low vegetation and defend a territory. Courtship and mating usually take place in the afternoon hours. Adults roost overnight on vegetation that has late afternoon exposure to the sun.

Papilio polyxenes asterius. Range in Florida: entire state. Maximum wingspread: 5 inches. Months seen: March through October, although it is sometimes seen in winter months. Generations per year: three. Caterpillar food: parsley, dill, fennel, anise, and other members of the carrot family.

INTRODUCTION TO SWALLOWTAILS

Swallowtails are among the largest and most beautiful of the Florida butterflies. They are so named because the long tails extending back from the hind wings in most species resemble the long tails of a swallow (all but the Polydamas). These tails divert birds' attention away from the butterfly's head, toward a part of its anatomy that is much more expendable, thus increasing its chance of surviving an attack by a hungry bird.

Swallowtails have other means of defense. Some species are distasteful to birds because their caterpillars feed on poisonous plants, and the butterflies advertise this by means of distinctive coloration. Several good-tasting species mimic the foul-tasting ones so

that predators will leave them alone as well.

Swallowtails are strong, swift flyers. When feeding, they usually open and close their wings if the flower is strong enough for them to perch. Otherwise, they hover, fluttering their wings rapidly, and grip the flower with their legs. In this manner, they balance themselves in mid-air while rapidly sucking up nectar. They move on to the next flower a few seconds later.

Swallowtails can live from two to three weeks when food is abundant. Some species, like the Schaus' Swallowtail live only a few days. Of the approximately 560 species of swallowtails worldwide, Florida has 10, more than any other state in the United States.

△ Eastern Black Swallowtail caterpillars, are green with black, yellow, and orange spots, although they look different in their different instars. Black Swallowtail and Giant Swallowtail caterpillars warn predators to "back off" by extending the colorful scent horns (osmeteria) located at the back of the head and sending a pungent odor into the air. Like their use of a silk girdle to hold their pupa upright on a stem, this trait is common to all swallowtails. The larvae of most swallowtails are smooth-skinned and all have an osmeterium.

The Eastern Black Swallowtail caterpillar is a common garden pest. It feeds on parsley and dill and is also called the parsley caterpillar.

△ The male of the Eastern Black Swallowtail has a wide row of yellow spots on the underside of both wings.

Swallowtails often have a large amount of black coloration. Black is useful because it absorbs heat better than other colors and helps the butterflies warm up. Most species in Florida have two noticeable tails. When a butterfly is in vigorous flight, it may be difficult to spot the small tails extending from the hindwing. However, the large size of Florida's 10 swallowtail species rules out any confusion with possible exception of the Monarch, which can easily be distinguished by its bright orange color.

▷ The female Eastern Black Swallowtail has very narrow yellow spots and expanded blue areas on the hindwings, causing it to have a closer resemblance than males to the Pipevine Swallowtail, another species that flies in the same areas.

Swallowtails

Family: Papilionidae

Zebra Swallowtail

The Zebra Swallowtail is the only U.S. representative of a tropical genus with many "kite-tailed" species, most of them predominantly white with black stripes and long tails. Tail length increases in successive generations during the year, reaching its maximum length in the fall brood.

The Zebra Swallowtail prefers woodlands along rivers and in swampy areas. But the adults also range widely into drier habitats in search of nectar sources and may even stray from the mainland into the upper Florida Keys. The caterpillar's food plant, pawpaw, is not found in the Keys. Adults may be seen flying in the woods or in scrub habitats along the Atlantic Coastal Ridge in South Florida. They are usually abundant and widespread.

Eurytites marcellus floridensis. Range in Florida: entire state, except the northern portion of northeastern Florida and the lower Florida Keys. Maximum wingspread: 4 inches. Months seen: March to December. Caterpillar food: pawpaws.

△ The Zebra Swallowtail is a familiar sight throughout Florida. The spring brood has very short tails, while the summer and fall broods have successively longer tails.

△ The Zebra Swallowtail caterpillar feeds on pawpaw leaves, a common plant which grows beneath the trees in Florida woodlands. Leaves are mostly fiber and water and don't have much food value. Therefore, larvae must eat huge quantities. However, leaves are usually plentiful.

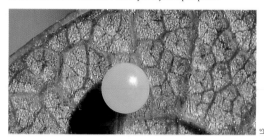

△ The egg of the Zebra Swallowtail is a pearly green sphere approximately one mm in diameter.

▷ A Zebra Swallowtail caterpillar prepares to pupate on a branch of its host plant.

60

△ The upperside of the Zebra Swallowtail shows the black and white, zebra-like stripes which inspired its name. Note the red marks on its hindwings.

The zebra-like patterns are believed to help deflect a predator's attention from the body and direct it backwards towards the less important tails, which could be snapped off by a bird's beak without impairing the survival of the butterfly itself. Spots on the tail end of the wings may aid in the deception by increasing its resemblance to a head.

The Zebra Longwing (page 24) is named for its long, narrow, black wings with yellow stripes. The Zebra Longwing is not related to the Zebra Swallowtail and the two species feed on entirely different plants.

◁ The stout, compact-looking chrysalis of the Zebra Swallowtail resembles a folded leaf. Swallowtails and sulphurs hang from a silk girdle when the caterpillar is forming a chrysalis. Other caterpillars hang from a silk pad attached to the branch. Although their larvae may spin a silk pad or silk girdle, very few species of butterflies spin silk cocoons around their pupae, although this is common among moths.

Like the pupa of other butterflies, the swallowtail's pupa splits open along sutures on either side, thus creating a flap. The butterfly pushes back the flap, crawls out at the top, and hangs downward waiting for its wings to dry.

Swallowtails

Family: Papilionidae

Spicebush Swallowtail

The scientific name of this butterfly, like that of many swallowtails, comes from the Homerian epic, the *Iliad*. Troilus was the son of Priam, King of Troy.

These butterflies love swamp forests and other semi-open situations where their caterpillars feed upon sassafras trees and spicebush.

The adults love nectar sources that have long, tubular or deep-throated, nectar-filled flowers such as Japanese honeysuckle, lantana, azalea and mimosa.

Males of the Spicebush Swallowtail may be found along woodland edges and roads, flying in search of females.

Papilio troilus. Range in Florida: entire state except southernmost tip of Dade County and the Florida Keys. Maximum wingspread: 5 inches. Months seen: March to December. Caterpillar food: spicebush, sassafras, and camphor tree.

△ Note the soft iridescent blue on the upperside of the Spicebush Swallowtail's wings and the single row of white dots. The flower is a buttonbush.

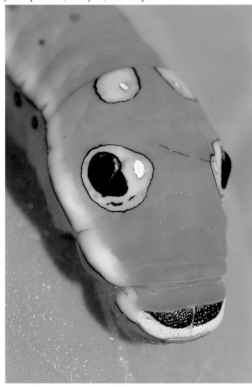

△ The later stages of the caterpillar of the Spicebush Swallowtail bear a striking resemblance to a small snake, although earlier stages resemble bird droppings. The large false eyes on each side of the expanded thorax complete the disguise. (See page 51 for details about their leaf-rolling behavior.)

Spicebush Swallowtail caterpillars look similar to those of the Palamedes Swallowtail, except for color. Both have false eyes and a snake-like appearance. Both also roll leaves to form shelters. The caterpillar pictured is a Spicebush.

Spicebush caterpillars feed on sassafras leaves with special fervor, but they occasionally eat the leaves of other forest shrubs and trees as well, such as the tulip tree, camphor tree and magnolia.

△ Wing patterns of the Spicebush Swallowtail resemble those of the foul-tasting Pipevine Swallowtail, helping to protect it against birds and other vertebrate predators, even though it is not actually distasteful.

Palamedes Swallowtail

The Palamedes Swallowtail is a large, blackish butterfly with a broad yellow band on each hindwing. Its tails are straight-sided and do not expand into a club shape, like those of the Giant Swallowtail. It is very abundant in wet woods near rivers on both coasts of Florida and across northern Florida but is rare in the Keys (where its larval food plants are not found). Adults love to visit thistles.

Many swallowtail species have names relating to ancient Greece. Palamedes was a hero of the Trojan War. Most of the swallowtail species in the US were discovered in the late 1700s, and scientists apparently followed a trend in choosing their names from classical literature.

Papilio palamedes. Range in Florida: entire state; strays found in the Florida Keys. Maximum wingspread: 5 inches. Months seen: March to December. Generations per year: three. Caterpillar food: the leaves of red bay and sweet bay trees.

△ The Palamedes Swallowtail caterpillar looks very much like a bird dropping in its early stages. The later stages have large eyespots on the thorax and mimic a snake to scare off predatory birds.

△ This remarkable photograph shows two Palamedes Swallowtails in flight. The male, slightly in front of the female, is gently enticing the female to land on the ground, preparatory to mating. With fluttering movements, he wafts scent from special scales on his wings to her antennae.

◁ Palamedes Swallowtails are a familiar sight throughout wooded areas in Florida and in gardens where they visit flowers such as pentas. This view shows the soft blue and orange spots on the underside that help it mimic the distasteful Pipevine Swallowtail for protection against birds.

Family: Papilionidae

Pipevine Swallowtail

The iridescent blue-green color and prominent tail of this species make the Pipevine Swallowtail very distinctive. This butterfly is also called the Blue Swallowtail because of its bluish iridescence.

The foul-tasting Pipevine Swallowtail is mimicked by six other butterflies in the eastern United States, including four that live in Florida (the Spicebush Swallowtail, the dark female form of the Eastern Tiger Swallowtail, the female Black Swallowtail, and the Red-spotted Purple).

Jane Brower, a Yale graduate student, demonstrated the effectiveness of this mimicry system in feeding experiments in Florida in 1958. She showed that birds avoid the palatable mimic species after they have tried to eat distasteful Pipevine Swallowtail adults.

The caterpillars feed on various species of the Pipevine (a vine with a peculiar flower, also known as Dutchman's Pipe, so-called because the shape of its flower resembles a smoker's pipe). Adults visit thistles, milkweeds, and many other flowers.

Battus philenor. Range in Florida: northern Florida to south central Florida, omitting only the southern tip and southeastern coast and the Florida Keys. Maximum wingspread: 4.5 inches. Months seen: February through November. Generations per year: three or four. Caterpillar food: pipevines (Aristolochia species).

▷ A Pipevine Swallowtail sipping nectar from a thistle plant. The red spots along the edges of its wings and its bright blue coloration warn passing birds to leave it alone because of its distasteful nature.

△ The Pipevine Swallowtail caterpillar is quite distasteful to birds because of chemicals contained in the leaves of the pipevines on which it feeds. Therefore, a number of edible swallowtails in Florida mimic the foul-tasting Pipevine for protection.

◁ The upperside of the Pipevine Swallowtail is quite attractive, with dark forewings and soft, iridescent bluish hindwings. Note the arrow-like shape of the white spots.

Eastern Tiger Swallowtail

Eastern Tiger Swallowtails are among the most famliar Florida butterflies. Their large size and yellow, black-striped wings make them instantly recognizable. Male Tigers fly along streams or woodland trails in search of females. They also visit mud puddles to drink water which contains minerals. Both sexes like to visit flowers such as milkweeds, thistles, and honeysuckle. The caterpillars feed on a variety of trees.

Papilio glaucus. Range in Florida: entire state except for extreme southern Dade County and the Florida Keys. Maximum wingspread: 6 inches. Months seen: mid-February to late October or November. Generations per year: three. Caterpillar food: tulip poplar, wild cherry, magnolia, sassafras, and other trees.

▷ The male Eastern Tiger Swallowtail shows the tiger-like stripes along the leading edge of its forewings which inspire its name. Note also the black stripe along its body.

△ Like other butterflies, the Tiger Swallowtail coils its long, tongue-like proboscis up to its face when it is not extended for drinking nectar.

◁ The Tiger Swallowtail caterpillar gains protection against its enemies by the large, false eyespots on the thorax. It also has an orange forked organ, the osmeterium, which can be extruded from the front of the thorax and which emits a very unpleasant odor.

TWO KINDS OF FEMALES

Besides the normal, four-striped, yellow female form, there is also an all-black, female Tiger Swallowtail which mimics the distasteful Pipevine Swallowtail for protection from predators. In areas where the dark Pipevine is common, black females predominate. In South Florida, the black form of the Tiger female is relatively rare. It is more common farther north where the Pipevine is more abundant. The yellow female form resembles the male (except for a more extensive blue area).

Swallowtails

Family: Papilionidae

Giant Swallowtail

The Giant Swallowtail is one of the largest butterflies in the United States, along with the Tiger Swallowtail and the Thoas Swallowtail (from Texas). The yellow spots on its dark brown wings are so distinctive that adults can be identified easily, even when in flight. Only in the Florida Keys can it be confused with two of its relatives, the Schaus Swallowtail and the Bahamian Swallowtail. However, its expanded, spoon-shaped tail has a large yellow spot in the center of its tip, unlike the Schaus Swallowtail, which has a straight tail with yellow along the outer edges rather than in the center.

The Giant Swallowtail is widely distributed across eastern North America, south into Cuba, and from northern South America up to Arizona and southeastern California. In Florida, it may be found in woody areas as well as citrus groves, where the females lay their eggs on new citrus leaves. It is also frequently seen in urban areas.

The first three caterpillar stages are black and white and strongly resemble bird droppings. The last two stages are brown with whitish patches on the tail end, around the middle, and on the sides of the forward portion of the body, and still bear a resemblance to bird droppings. The caterpillars have a bright red-orange forked organ, called an osmeterium, which emits a noxious odor composed of various organic acids. They stick out these scent horns, or stink glands, as they are sometimes called, to help repel ants or other potential predators that may try to attack them.

The pupa is mottled brown and resembles a piece of wood. The upper half is suspended slightly away from the tree branch by a silken girdle. The bottom of the pupa is attached to a little silk button on the tree.

Papilio cresphontes. Range in Florida: entire state. Maximum wingspread: 5 inches or so. Months seen: every month. Caterpillar food: citrus tree leaves, wild lime, and torchwood.

△△ The broken pattern on the underside of its wings helps conceal the Giant Swallowtail from predators.
△ From above, the Giant Swallowtail looks like dappled sunlight hitting a dark leaf, and its wing outline is broken up appropriately.

◁ The caterpillar of the Giant Swallowtail, commonly called the Orange Dog, is a minor agricultural pest; it feeds on the leaves of young citrus trees. It resembles a bird dropping in all its five stages.

Like other members of the swallowtail family, the Giant Swallowtail caterpillar repels predators by extruding its osmeterium (scent horns) and emitting a strong, unpleasant odor. It may also wipe the fluid from the outside of its scent horns onto an inquisitive ant or other potential predator.

Polydamas Swallowtail

This is the only swallowtail in Florida that lacks tails. This distinctive swallowtail is all black on the upper side, except for a row of yellow chevrons or spots near the margin of the wing. Underneath, there is a row of wavy red lines.

The adults prefer open areas, particularly old fields and suburban planted areas or open pine woods. Adults are rather long-lived for butterflies; marked specimens have been found up to 27 days after they were released. This butterfly is sometimes abundant near sandy ocean beaches in the Keys or on the mainland of Florida. Adults are often locally common near patches of the larval foodplants, pipevines.

Battus polydamus lucaus. Range in Florida: entire state except for the drier south-central portions. Maximum wingspread: 5 inches. Months seen: early April through November. Generations per year: three (possibly two). Caterpillar food: pipevines.

△ Polydamas Swallowtail drinking nectar on lantana. This is the only swallowtail in Florida without tails. Note the single yellow band and the heavily scalloped hindwings.

△ The underside of the Polydamas Swallowtail is marked somewhat like that of the Pipevine Swallowtail, a close relative, and both are protected from birds by poisonous compounds in their bodies.

◁ The Polydamas Swallowtail caterpillar is a glistening, dull-reddish color with several rows of orange, fleshy tubercles. When young, the caterpillars live in groups, but they become more solitary in their last several stages. When annoyed, they may stick out a yellow horn (osmeterium) and emit a foul odor. They feed on pipevines and are distasteful to birds, lizards, and some of the other potential predators.

△ The Polydamas Swallowtail pupa resembles a twisted green leaf as it hangs suspended from the stem of a pipevine.

Swallowtails

Family: Papilionidae

Schaus Swallowtail

The Schaus Swallowtail, Florida's rarest resident butterfly, is justly famous around the world as an endangered species. Its range once stretched from south Miami in Dade County to the southern tip of the Florida Keys, but today it is restricted to three or four tiny islands in Biscayne National Park and the extreme northern tip of Key Largo. It has precariously survived in this final stronghold since 1972, the last year that it was abundant across most of Key Largo. Its loss throughout the Keys and on the mainland was caused first by habitat destruction because of the ever-increasing human population and subsequently by mosquito-control spraying throughout the Keys. In 1972, Monroe County began using Dibrom and Baytex, two pesticides that are particularly potent against butterflies. Baytex was later taken off the market, but Dibrom is still in use in Florida mosquito-control programs.

The Schaus Swallowtail resembles the Giant Swallowtail with its dark yellow pattern on a dark brown background, but it has a large reddish-brown patch and a row of diffuse, blue spots on the underside of the hindwing. Together with its straight-sided tail, marked with yellow along the outer edge, the Schaus species is quite distinctive. In flight, the Schaus Swallowtail moves very slowly and may actually hover or even fly backwards, much like a Zebra Longwing. Tropical hardwood hammocks are its favored habitat. The adults emerge in April or May at the beginning of the wet season. Males patrol along hammock edges and trails, while females usually fly within the hammock, searching for wild lime and torchwood, upon which they lay their eggs.

Papilio aristodemus ponceanus. Range: upper Florida Keys. Maximum wingspread: about 4 inches. Months seen: April or May until late June. Generations per year: one. Caterpillar food: wild lime and torchwood.

△ The mature larva is camouflaged by a series of white blotches on an olive-green to brown background. A series of blue dots along its side and back immediately distinguish it from the rather similar Giant Swallowtail larva. Additionally, the larval horn (osmeterium), when extended from behind the head, is white.

△ The adult Schaus Swallowtail can be identified immediately by its tail, which is bordered with yellow on the upperside. The magenta purple patch on the underside of the wings, bounded by iridescent baby blue, is also very distinctive.

AN EXPERIMENT IN CAPTIVE BREEDING AND REINTRODUCTION INTO THE WILD

An elaborate program to bring the Schaus Swallowtail butterfly back from the edge of extinction has been underway at the Boender Endangered Species Laboratory at the University of Florida since 1992, when Hurricane Andrew destroyed virtually all of the Schaus' wild habitat. While the habitat is recovering, this endangered butterfly is being cultured by the author of this book, Dr. Thomas Emmel, and his graduate students.

Eggs were removed from wild populations in the northern Florida Keys and brought to Gainesville where the caterpillars were raised on wild lime trees and torchwood trees, the species' native food plants, until they reached the fifth stage (instar) of development. At that stage, they were transferred to cups because they begin to wander about looking for a place to pupate. Confined within a cup, with a doctor's wooden tongue depressor inside, the larva usually formed its pupa on the wooden stick. This stick, with the pupa attached, would be transferred to a tree in the Florida Keys, where the adult would finally emerge.

By 1994, the captive colony had grown to the point where thousands of eggs, larvae, and pupae were being produced.

The first reintroductions of this species ever attempted were carried out in 1995 and 1996. Selected sites in the Upper, Middle, and Lower Keys were identified and pupae were released in the early spring. There the adults emerged under natural conditions. They remained in the area, mated, and reproduced on their native hosts of torchwood and wild lime.

The success of this program will be measured by the fate of the newly established wild populations. To date, they are doing very well. To increase the chance this species will survive in the wild, it has been reintroduced to many parts of its former range, not just its presently restricted range in Biscayne National Park.

Supported by the U.S. Fish & Wildlife Service and the Nongame Wildlife Program of the Florida Game and Fresh Water Fish Commission, this is the largest captive-breeding program ever undertaken on behalf of an endangered species of invertebrate.

Geometrid Moths

Family: Geometridae

Worldwide, this is one of the largest moth families, although the size of the individual moths is not so large. Geometrid caterpillars advance by pulling their tails forward as they arch their backs and then extend their bodies toward the head. Thus, they have earned the name Inchworm.

▷ Geometrid Moths have sharply angled forewings. *(Leptostales hepaticaria)*

▽ Green Geometrid Moths, such as this species *(Nemorialixaria)* from Lake County, Florida are well concealed in their daytime resting places on lichens and other green plant growth.

INTRODUCTION TO MOTHS

Moths, like butterflies, belong to the great insect order Lepidoptera. With 120,000 named species worldwide, Lepidoptera are second in number of species only to Coleoptera, the beetles.

Moths have four wings which are covered with scales. These scales, which are greatly expanded hairs, produce a marvelous array of colors and patterns on the wings of the adults.

Not all moths are plain or dull-colored. Some moths, like the Luna, are as beautiful as any butterfly. At one time, the wings of the most colorful moths were made into fashion jewelry. Some of the more notable Florida moths are described on the following pages.

THE INCHWORM

Geometrid Moth caterpillars are called *Measuring Worms, Inchworms, or Loopers.* *They have fewer pairs of legs than other caterpillars. Instead of moving with the wave-like leg motion of most caterpillars, loopers arch their bodies, drawing their rear end forward, and then extending the front section, thus inching along.*

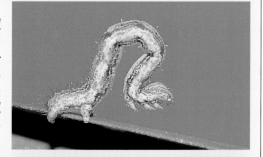

△ *This Geometrid Moth larva has attached bits of flower to itself for camouflage.*

△ *This inchworm has extended its body in a straight, twig-like shape for camouflage.*

Underwing Moths

Family: Noctuidae

The caterpillars of these usually dull-patterned moths are sometimes called "cutworms," because some species cut through plant stems. Some are serious agricultural pests. One group of Noctuids, the underwing moths, may appear dull with their wings folded, but when these wings are opened, the hind wings show exceptionally brilliant colors. North Florida has the greatest diversity of underwing moths in the world, mostly because there are so many hardwoods and pines which serve as host plants for the larvae. A collection could be put together from just the underwings found at porchlights that would be the envy of any lepidopterist in the world.

Darling Underwing

The Darling Underwing Moth (shown at top) has very dull, camouflaged forewings, but its brilliantly-colored hindwings are exposed when it is startled or it takes flight, hence the name "underwing." This sudden flash of unexpected color probably surprises predators and may cause them to momentarily lose their composure. This diversion may save the moth from being eaten.

Catocala cara. Range: Florida to Canada. Maximum wingspread: 2.9-3.3 inches. Months seen: August to October. Caterpillar food: willows and poplars.

THE DIFFERENCES BETWEEN BUTTERFLIES AND MOTHS

Day versus Night: *Most butterflies fly during the day and have bright colors. Most moths fly at night and many have drab colors, especially on the underside of their wings. Moths need drab colors so that they can remain camouflaged when they are resting during the daylight hours. Many of the day-flying moths have brighter colors.*

Different Antennae: *Butterfly antennae are usually slender and have knobs at the tips which are known as clubs. Moths have tapered or wide, feathery antennae. Their antennae do not have "clubs" at the tips like those of the butterflies.*

How They Fold Their Wings: *When at rest, most butterflies hold their wings folded together vertically above their bodies. Butterflies usually have bright colors on the tops of their wings and duller colors underneath. This helps them camouflage themselves while at rest by exposing only the dull color. Moths, on the other hand, rest with their wings extended horizontally, wrapped around their bodies, or pressed against the support on which they are resting. Moths generally have dull colors both above and beneath their wings.*

Warming Up: *Moths raise their body temperatures to flying condition by "shivering" their muscles, whereas butterflies generally warm up by basking in the sun and absorbing solar radiation.*

Body Shape and Scales: *Butterflies tend to have slender bodies in comparison to the size of their wings. Their scales are pressed tightly against their wings, forming a smooth surface. Also, the scales on their bodies give a smooth appearance. Moths have stout bodies and their scales give them a furry appearance, both on their bodies and their wings.*

Sense of Smell: *Butterflies smell with sensors in their feet and with their antennae. Moths smell with their antennae only. Moths find their mates in the dark with sexual perfumes.*

Frenulum: *Moths have a structure called a frenulum which connects their front and back wings. Butterfly front and hind wings overlap but are not connected by such a hook.*

Moths Are Much More Numerous: *North of Mexico, there are over 700 species of butterflies in North America, but there are more than ten times as many species of moths and the moths are far more diverse in form, structure, and choice of larval foodplants.*

The above differences apply to most butterflies and moths, but for some of these rules, there are many exceptions.

Noctuid Moths

Family Noctuidae
Spanish Moth

The Spanish Moth shown in the photo is an adult, clinging, during daytime, to the bark of a tree in Everglades National Park. Most nocturnal moths, gaudy as they may seem around lights at night, are actually rather cryptically colored (well-camouflaged) in their chosen daytime resting places.

The Spanish moth has a distinctive, hairy black body with striking pink and black forewings, although its hindwings are plain and dark.

Xanthopastis timais. Wingspan: 1 1/2 to 1 3/4 inches. Months seen: November through May. Caterpillar food: figs and spider lily.

THE WORLD OF MICRO-MOTHS

The smallest moths in the world have wingspans of less than one-half of an inch. These small creatures are far more numerous than their larger relatives. However, they are the least known of all moths. They are difficult to study because of their small size. Probably less than two dozen scientists in the entire world specialize in micro-moths. Yet their are almost 100 families, each with its own fascinating, but hidden, natural history. Most of the new species of moths discovered in the future will probably be micro-moths and new discoveries about moth behavior will probably also be in this field.

◁ *Some micro-moths are as beautiful as the gaudiest butterflies. This specimen (photographed in California) sports ultra-long antennae which serve the same purpose as the wide, feathery antennae of the Saturnids. The large surface area provides room for a huge number of scent receptors.*

THE FATAL ATTRACTION OF MOTHS (WHY MOTHS FLY INTO LIGHTS)

Everyone has seen a moth singe its wings in a candle's flame or senselessly fling itself against a light bulb. This apparent self-destruction is beyond the moth's control. Moths that fly during the night navigate by using the light from the moon and stars while day-flying moths rely on the sun's rays. By flying at a fixed angle to a distant light source such as the moon, the moth can navigate a straight path, because the light rays always come from the same direction. However, if a moth approaches a light source which is very close, such as a street lamp, the moth becomes confused because the light rays radiate in all directions. The moth vainly tries to fly at a constant angle to the light, but since the light is so close, the light appears to come from a constantly changing direction as the moth moves. *The moth must constantly turn to keep aligned at the same angle. It finds itself circling the light and spiraling closer and closer to its doom. The navigational skills that enable the moth to make use of nature's light sources are not designed to work with man-made lights.*

▷ *From a very distant light source such as the sun or moon, all rays appear to be almost parallel regardless of the movement of the moth. By flying at a constant angle to the rays, the moth can travel in a straight line. When the light source is very close (a few feet away), even small changes in the moth's position means that the light will be coming from a different direction, requiring the moth to constantly change its course to maintain the same angle with the light rays.*

Wasp Moths

Family: Arctiidae
Subfamily: Ctenuchidae

Wasp moths are brightly colored, day-flying moths. Wasp moths look like wasps and thus gain protection from their enemies. For some species the mimicry includes imitation of wasp movement and flight, while for others it includes resting in the position that a wasp assumes when feeding on flower pollen. Their narrow wings and daytime activity make these moths very noticeable. Their imitation of wasps is important for their survival; since they fly during the daytime, they would be more vulnerable to predators such as birds otherwise. In addition to their wasp mimicry, the larvae of certain species feed on toxic plants such as oleander. The toxic chemicals may be passed on to the adults, making them distasteful to predators.

Oleander Moth

The Oleander Moth or Polka-dot Wasp Moth (sometimes called the Uncle Sam Moth because of its red, white, and blue colors), is a very distinctive day-flying wasp moth. It has dark, metallic-blue wings with white spots. Its body is also metallic-blue, and the abdomen has a pair of white spots at its base, with a red tip. The larva feeds on oleander, a popular, widely planted flowering shrub. The highly poisonous oleander plant is shunned by most caterpillars, but this species feasts on the leaves and is probably protected by the poisons it ingests. Its distinctive colors may serve to advertise its distastefulness to potential predators. It can be found all over Florida, especially in the tourist areas of South Florida and Orlando where oleander has been widely planted as an ornamental.

Syntomeida epilias. Range in Florida: central and southern Florida (wherever oleander is planted). Months seen: all months. Caterpillar food: oleander and devil's potato.

△ The caterpillar of the Oleander Moth feeding on oleander, a host plant imported from the Old World tropics.

Scarlet-bodied Wasp Moth

This moth gains protection from potential predators by looking like a wasp, though it is actually a tasty moth.

Cosmosoma myrodora. Range in Florida: entire state. When seen: entire year in South Florida, April to November in North Florida. Caterpillar food: climbing hempweed.

Sphinx Moths

Family: Sphingidae

These moths were given the name "sphinx moth" because the caterpillar, in its resting position, with the front part of its body raised in the air, was thought to resemble the Great Sphinx of Egypt. Sphinx moths are also called hawk moths because their wings resemble hawks' wings in shape, and because of their strong flight and hovering ability. They can attain airspeeds of up to 25 mph. Their wings beat almost as fast as those of hummingbirds.

The abdomen of a sphinx moth usually tapers down to a sharp point. The forewings are much larger than the small, triangular-shaped hind wings, and the antennae are usually thicker in the middle.

Banded Sphinx Moth

This moth, resting on a cassia plant in the photo at right, shows the disruptive marks that help conceal it from predators during the daytime.

Eumorpha fasciata. Range in Florida: entire state. When seen: May to July, August to November (two broods). Wingspan: 3.5-4.2 inches. Caterpillar food: evening primrose.

Tersa Sphinx Moth

The adult Tersa Sphinx Moth is one of the most slender and streamlined of the hawk moths. Like a number of sphinx moth species, it has earth-tone colors and an extremely long and pointed body. This day-flying moth can be found at flowers.

Tersa Sphinx caterpillars have large eyespots behind the head. When disturbed, the caterpillar tucks its head, causing the eyespots to be more prominent. The result is an excellent imitation of a snake.

Xylophanes tersa. Range in Florida: entire state. Months seen: February through November. Wingspan: 5 to 6 inches. Caterpillar food: Manettia species, smooth button plant, and starcluster.

△ Sphinx moth caterpillars almost always have a large horn at the tip of the abdomen but are otherwise naked, without hairs or other physical ornamentation. Most Sphinx Moth caterpillars pupate in the soil and the pupae have a jug-like form. There are many species of sphinx moths in Florida, including some tropical species from the West Indies with a very limited range in this state. Tobacco and tomato hornworms are part of the sphinx moth group.

▽ The snake-like caterpillar of the Hog Sphinx (*Darapsa myron*) has frightening eyespots on either side of the thorax. This caterpillar can retract the first two segments of its body into the third segment, which is enlarged to allow this behavior. The moth's name comes from its caterpillar's resemblance to a hog's jowls and snout.

△ This photo shows a White-lined Sphinx Moth (*Hyles lineata*) feeding, in flight, on blazing star flowers. Sphinx moths, like hummingbirds, extract nectar while hovering in front of deep-throated flowers. Their powerful wings beat so rapidly they make a humming sound. The tongue is usually well developed and may be extremely long in sphinx species, sometimes twice the body length. They are most often seen drinking nectar in this manner at twilight and may be mistaken for hummingbirds. While sipping nectar, the head and tongue are dusted by pollen which may be transferred to the next flower. They are usually attracted to pale-colored flowers.

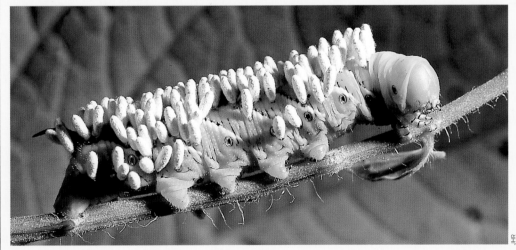

WASPS VERSUS MOTHS

This photo shows a sphinx moth caterpillar covered with the larva cocoons of the parasitic Braconid Wasp. The female wasp first laid small eggs on the caterpillar. When the wasp larvae hatched, they began making a meal of the caterpillar but only ate non-vital tissues until they completed their growth. They then spun their cocoons on the outside of the caterpillar to complete their development into scores of new Braconid Wasps. Many moths and butterflies are vulnerable to this method used by certain wasps and flies to provide a sure supply of food for their offspring.

Some caterpillars have evolved strategies to defend themselves against parasites such as wasps. Caterpillars of the Gulf Fritallary, Zebra Longwing, and Buckeye Butterflies have long spines on their bodies which prevent many parasites from laying eggs. The egg-laying tube of the female wasp is not long enough to reach the skin from the top of the spines on which she lands.

Monarch, Queen, and Pipevine Swallowtail caterpillars have fleshy appendages on their bodies which they whip about to deter wasps from landing. They swish these appendages in the same manner that a horse shoos flies away with its tail. Other caterpillars violently thrash their bodies to deter wasps. Many moth caterpillars are covered with long hairs to deter parasites.

Giant Silkmoths

Family: Saturniidae

Most of the giant silkmoths spin silk cocoons, although their silk is usually not as fine as that of the Silk Moth (*Bombyx mori*) which is bred commercially for its silk, and which survives in domesticated culture but no longer exists in the wild. A few other giant silkmoths are bred commercially for their silk, but none are Florida species.

The caterpillars of Giant Silkmoths are among the most colorful and spectacular of all caterpillars in their decorative markings. A good example is the extraordinary caterpillar of the Io Moth.

Io Moth

The Io Moth is easily recognized by the beautiful, white-centered eyespot on its hindwing. This may be the origin of its name, as the eyespot is a bit moon-like, and Io is one of the moons of the planet Jupiter. The eyespot also resembles a bull's-eye, so this moth is sometimes called the Bull's-eye Moth. The larvae, equipped with sharp stinging spines which can penetrate human flesh, feed on many plants, including maples, oaks, willows, clover, and corn.

Automeris io. Range in Florida: entire state. Wingspread: up to 3 inches. Months seen: May to September. Generations per year: several. Caterpillar food: leaves of oaks, maples, willows and other trees.

△ The Io Moth opens its wings wide, in a threat display, to reveal the eyespots on the hindwings which resemble a face. This is a male Io Moth. Males have a rich yellow coloration. Compare the reddish female shown on the opposite page.

△ This close-up view of the male Io Moth shows the feather-like antennae extending from the head. These antennae are the source of the moth's incredible sense of smell, allowing it to detect and locate mates more than one mile away.

△ Notice the stinging spines on this Io Moth caterpillar and its defensive position. It is curled around the stem of a plant so that its spines face outward towards any potential predator, providing protection from every angle. The Io Moth has barbed hairs which can irritate human skin. Other well-known stinging caterpillars are the Saddleback Moth caterpillar, the Puss Moth caterpillar, and the caterpillar of the Hag Moth. Some caterpillars have spines which are connected to a central reservoir of poison. Others have hairs which have been rubbed in poisonous fecal matter.

Although Io Moths have protective hairs which are painful to humans, they are still vulnerable to Ichneumon Wasps which destroy large numbers of Io Moths by laying eggs on the caterpillars. When the eggs hatch, the wasp larvae bore inside and feed on the caterpillars. Other parasitic wasps destroy caterpillars by injecting their eggs into them rather than laying eggs upon them.

▽ Io Moths, male (yellow) and female (reddish brown forewings), with wings spread in threat display, showing how the eyespots of the hindwing can be flashed to frighten predators.

Giant Silk Moths

Family: Saturniidae

Cecropia Moth

The Cecropia Moth is easily recognized by its large size and its red body with white collar and white banding across the abdomen. With a wingspan of up to six inches, this is the largest moth in North America. The wings are dark brownish with red shading towards the body.

The caterpillar feeds on many trees and shrubs, including maples, poplars, and willows. It forms a spindle-shaped cocoon of loose brown silk, attached lengthwise to a twig, which is readily visible in winter.

This moth was named after Kekrops, an ancient king who was the legendary founder of Athens.

Hyalophora cecropia. Range in Florida: northern part of the state (infrequently encountered). Maximum wingspread: 6 inches. Months seen: May to July. Generations per year: one. Caterpillar food: maples, poplars, and willows.

△ Male Cecropia Moths have huge, feathery antennae.

▷ A Cecropia Moth hangs from a fern in the evening, preparing to take flight.

△△ At top, a close-up view of the Cecropia Moth caterpillar, showing the remarkable tubercles behind its head. Due to its fierce-looking spines and tubercles, most potential predators would probably leave this caterpillar alone.

△ With a wingspan of 4 to 6 inches, the male Cecropia Moth is the largest moth in North America.

Giant Silkmoths

Family: Saturniidae

Imperial Moth

The yellow wings of the Imperial Moth have varying amounts of purple or pink spotting. Its caterpillars also occur in several color forms which are called phases.

The eggs of the Imperial Moth have an interesting concave shape. They can be gathered from a gravid (fertilized) female by confining her in a paper sack overnight. The next morning, the eggs will be found inside the bag, glued to the paper.

Eacles imperialis. Range in Florida: entire state. Months seen: all year, but greater numbers appear from April to September. Caterpillar food: maple, basswood, walnut, and other tree leaves.

△ The female of the Imperial Moth (above) has more yellow on its wings than the male. It also has smaller antennae. The male Imperial Moth (left) is one of the largest silkmoths in Florida. It has much more purple on its wings than the female. It also has very large, feathery antennae.

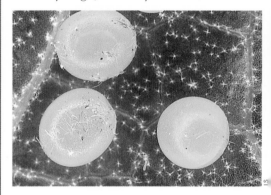

△ The large eggs of the Imperial Moth are somewhat depressed in the center.

△ These three caterpillars, although very different in color, are all Imperial Moths. They occur in several color forms (scientifically called phases, although the caterpillars do not change colors). Used in this manner, the term "phase" refers not a passing stage, but to a sub-group that differs in appearance from other members of the same species. Shown here, from left to right, are the green phase, the brown phase, and the reddish-orange phase. Note that the line of oval markings remains similar.

Luna Moth

The Luna Moth is one of Florida's most spectacular moths. Its pale green wings and the long sweeping tails of the hindwings are especially beautiful. There is a transparent, moon-shaped spot on each wing which accounts for its name.

Luna Moths and their relatives are members of the giant silkmoth family, a group which includes the largest moths. The adults of this group never eat but survive on nutrients the caterpillars stored. They fly, mate, find a host plant, lay their eggs, and die, all in a brief lifespan of about three days.

Luna Moth caterpillars pupate on the ground inside a cocoon which is concealed among leaf litter. The caterpillars spend the winter in their cocoons and the adults emerge in the spring. Silk for fabric is collected from the cocoons of certain species of this group.

Female Luna Moths produce chemical attractants called pheromones in the scent scales on their wings. The males detect these perfumes with their large, feathery antennae, at distances of a mile or more.

Actias luna. Wingspread: 3 to 4.5 inches. Range in Florida: North Florida. Months seen: January to November. Generations per year: three or four. Caterpillar food: hickories, sweet gum, and pecan, and many other forest trees.

▷ The Luna Moth adult is a familiar sight around lights at night and resting on vegetation in North Florida, especially in early spring, although it is relatively common most months of the year.

△ The larva of the Luna Moth feeds on many different forest trees in Florida.

▷ This posture is a threat display. The forewings are spread to reveal the two eyespots.

81

Giant Silkmoths

Family: Saturniidae

Polyphemus Moth

The Polyphemus Moth is named after Polyphemus, the one-eyed giant of Greek mythology. This moth has a large, oval, transparent eyespot edged with yellow, blue, and black.

The Polyphemus Moth is relatively common throughout Florida. It usually spends the winter in its cocoon, but warm temperatures in January or February may cause it to emerge. Because of Florida's mild weather, it may be seen at any time of the year although most adults emerge from their cocoons after March.

Polyphemus Moths are frequently seen at night around street lights.

Antheraea polyphemus. Range in Florida: entire state. Maximum wingspan: 6 inches. Months seen: all year. Caterpillar food: trees and shrubs, including hickories, maples, oaks and pines.

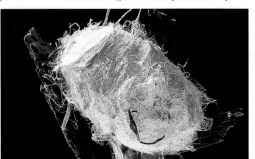

◁ The silken cocoon of the Polyphemus Moth hangs from the host plant and is fairly easily found in the winter. The cocoon conceals a hard, brown pupa. If a cocoon is gathered and brought inside, the entire family may enjoy watching the adult moth emerge in the spring.

△ This close-up photo shows the modified scales of the moth's body which make it very furry and significantly different from the body of of butterflies. the moth's body scales are greatly eongated, almost like hairs, in contrast to the short, flat, shingle-like scales and a butterfly's body or wing.

△ This male Polyphemus Moth sports the large, feathery antennae characteristic of males of the silkmoth family. These sensitive, complex antennae can detect the odor of a female moth as much as several miles away, even though the female releases only one billionth of a gram of her perfume per hour. One reason the moth's scent-detecting apparatus is so effective is that each antenna has 1,700 hairs, and each hair has several thousand scent-detecting pores. Each pore is specifically designed to detect the pheremone (scent) of the female of that particular species. In this manner, the sensitivity of the pores is multiplied more than one million times, enabling the male moth to find his mate over long distances.

THE MOTH GARDEN

At night, as butterflies find places to roost, usually on tall grasses or under leaves, moths take over the night shift in the garden. Different species become active at different times during the night, some beginning at dusk, others much later.

Many butterfly lovers develop an interest in moths because of their tremendous variety. There are more than ten times as many moth species as butterfly species. Many moths seek nectar from flowers the same as butterflies and indeed visit many of the same flowers. Of particular interest to moths in Florida are white petunia, yellow honeysuckle, and white impatiens.

The moth gardener in Florida can hope to attract sphinx moths, primarily. Some moths, such as the silk moths, do not seek nectar because they lack mouth parts. They do not feed and live their entire lives (a week or so) on energy from food stored as a caterpillar. However, they can be attracted to gardens with the appropriate food plants for their caterpillars. They come looking for places to lay their eggs rather than places to feed.

One difference in feeding behavior between moths and butterflies is that moths usually do not land on flowers. They take their nectar hummingbird-style, while hovering. Moths are also attracted to sap running from trees. This can be simulated by preparing a paste from beer and brown sugar and smearing it on the bark of trees to attract moths. Some recipes include fruit, such as mashed ripe bananas and yeast. The mixture may be even more effective after it has been left to ferment for a few days.

Moths are not as important as butterflies for pollination of most flowers, but some species of flowers can only be pollinated by moths. For example, the yucca can only be pollinated by the Yucca Moth (see page 56). Certain tropical flowers are pollinated only by sphinx moths because their deep nectaries can only be reached by the sphinx moth's ultra-long tongue (up to 10 inches in some species).

To observe moths, it is best not to turn on bright lights which might distract them (especially the males). It is better to use a flashlight with a piece of yellow or red plastic as a filter.

Remove ultraviolet bug zappers to improve moth populations in a garden. These devices have been discredited for mosquito control, but they do attract and kill large numbers of harmless moths.

Giant Silkmoths

Family: Saturniidae

Royal Walnut Moth

The Royal Walnut Moth, also known as the Regal Moth, is a large moth with a wingspan of five to six inches. Its most striking feature is its orange-red wing veins and yellow markings which appear on a dark background.

Citheronia regalis. Range: North Florida. Wingspread: 3.8 to 6.2 inches. Months seen: June to September (one brood). Caterpillar food: walnut and hickory leaves.

△ This head-on view of a Royal Walnut Moth shows the soft, beautiful, hair-like scales on its thorax and rest of its body. These scales make it possible for moths to be active at night in cool temperatures. The thick pile of scaling insulates the moth's body, which is warmed by muscle shivering prior to taking flight.

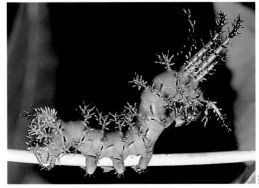

△ The Royal Walnut Moth has a strangely-shaped, camouflage-colored larva which may grow up to six inches in length. The head of this bizarre-looking caterpillar is adorned with large spines and spiky black and orange horns, but it is totally harmless. However, it presents a frightening appearance to would-be predators. Its food plants include walnut trees; hence the common name of the adult. It eats hickory leaves as well, and is also commonly called the Hickory Horned Devil.

Rosy Maple Moth

This Rosy Maple Moth seems to be deliberately advertising its presence by its position on the bark, but to a bird it probably looks like a yellowing or decaying leaf.

The caterpillar of this moth is known as the Green-striped Mapleworm. It feeds primarily on the leaves of maple trees, as its name suggests, but it is also found on oaks.

Adult Rosy Maple Moths occur in different color forms. The usual form has bright pink forewings, as shown above, but there is also a white form found in the Midwest.

Dryocampa rubicunda. Range in Florida: North Florida. Months seen: April to September (two broods). Wingspread: 1.4-2.1 inches. Caterpillar food: leaves of maples and oaks.

PROTECTIVE COLORATION

Butterflies and moths demonstrate the different ways in which protective coloration is employed by prey species for protection against predators. In fact, in their use of protective coloration, insects probably exhibit greater diversity and finer detail than any other animal group. This is not really surprising, considering that there are far more insect species than all other kinds of animals combined.

Cryptic Coloration

Perhaps the most common type of protective coloration is cryptic coloration, where the insect resembles an object or background in its environment so well that the insect is camouflaged or hidden from view. A moth, for example, may resemble a leaf or the bark of the tree trunk on which it rests, and a swallowtail caterpillar may resemble a bird dropping. The elaborate patterns and colors which help an insect resemble its background presumably have evolved over thousands of generations through natural selection. Individuals that did not effectively resemble their background were more likely to be spotted by predators, while those that were better concealed were more likely to survive and pass on their genes to their progeny.

Warning Coloration

Some prey animals survive, on the other hand, not by hiding but by wearing a sign that says "I'm bad; don't mess with me!" These animals employ warning coloration to advertise that they are distasteful or otherwise noxious or dangerous, so that most predators will not attempt to eat them but will be warned off by the conspicuous colors. Bright colors, such as red, orange, yellow, and black stripes, are typically used for this purpose. Hence, warning coloration is sometimes called aposematic coloration, meaning "standing out against the norm." The Monarch butterfly is a well-known example of warning coloration.

For such coloration to be effective, predators must be capable of learning from experience to avoid such conspicuously colored prey, or they must develop an instinctive aversion to certain colors and patterns through evolution.

Frightening Coloration

Frightening coloration involves the use of large eyespots, as on the Io Moth adult or the front end of the Sphinx Moth caterpillar, to fool a small predator, such as a bird or lizard, into thinking the edible prey is much larger or more dangerous than it really is.

△ The perfect camouflage of the twig-like caterpillar of the Geometrid Moth.

▷ The frightening, snake-like markings of the caterpillar of the Tersa Sphinx Moth.

△ The eyespots on the wings of the Io Moth produce the illusion of a face, which may be enough to startle some predators.

▷ A geometrid larva on dog fennel. This larva has covered itself with camouflage materials from its host plant.

Tent Caterpillar Moths

Family: Lasiocampidae

Eastern Tent Caterpillar Moth

Tent Caterpillar Moths are medium-sized moths with large, hairy bodies in comparison to the size of their wings. Adults lack a functional proboscis and do not feed during their short life. Relatively dull in color and uninteresting in pattern, the adults of this group do not attract much attention. However, the larvae are striped lengthwise, quite colorful, and very hairy.

Some species of tent caterpillars are serious pests on shade trees and in hardwood forests. The larvae build communal webs (tents) in trees for protection from predators. They leave these tents during the night to feed on the foliage of the host tree and other nearby trees and then return to the tent to pass the day. Pupation is done inside a cocoon. The large number of caterpillars that emerge from the tent can defoliate a tree within a few days. The unsightly tents and the damage caused by the caterpillars make these serious pests for many homeowners and foresters.

Malacosoma americana. Range in Florida: North Florida. Months seen: May to June. Maximum wingspan: 0.9-1.8 inches. Caterpillar food: apple and cherry trees, crabapples, and other members of the rose family.

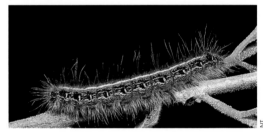

△ The Eastern Tent Caterpillar is rather attractive, but it is a severe pest responsible for defoliating many trees each spring.

Eastern Tent Caterpillars make a silken tent around branches of trees. The scene in the top photo is frequently encountered in the woodlands of Florida in the spring. The silk resembles a spider's web and is produced by spinnerets located near the caterpillar's mouth. One female moth lays a cluster of eggs in midsummer. When the eggs hatch the following spring, the caterpillars work together to spin a tent that serves as a shelter when they are not out on the branches of the tree feeding on the foliage.

Fall Webworm   ▷
Family: Arctiidae

By comparison, the Fall Webworm creates the much larger web shown at right. Small trees may be entirely covered with the spiderweb-like material.

Hyphantria cunea. Range in Florida: North Florida. Months seen: April to September: Maximum wingspan: 1.0-1.6 inches. Caterpillar food: over 100 species of trees, including hickory, oak, maple, and walnut.

Family: Zygaenoidea

Saddleback Caterpillar Moth

The Saddleback Caterpillar Moth is a relatively inconspicuous, glossy, dark chocolate-brown moth in the adult stage. However, the colorful larva is encountered more commonly than the adult and makes an unforgettable impression on a person unfortunate enough to be stung by the poisonous bristles on its body.

The caterpillar is named for the dark-brown, saddle-shaped patch bordered with white in the center of its back.

Sibine stimulea. Range in Florida: entire state. Months seen: June and July. Caterpillars feed on apple trees, blueberries, citrus, corn, dogwoods, maples, oaks, and palms.

▷ The Saddleback Caterpillar moth, shown here on ixora, gives little hint of the poisonous nature of its caterpillar.

▽ The Saddleback Caterpillar has numerous stinging spines on its body. These spines inject poison and cause intense pain if someone accidentally brushes against them, even lightly. Unfortunately, there is no known remedy short of general anesthesia. If stung, here is the advice of experts: "Scream for Momma! Hold wounded body part tightly and wait half an hour, or so, for the intense pain to go away." Better to just avoid touching this beautiful creature.

BUTTERFLIES AND MOTHS AS SPIRITS

Because they are so beautiful and soar so freely, many cultures have regarded butterflies and moths a symbols of the human soul. Their miraculous change from caterpillar to winged adult, after spending time in the coffin-like chamber of the chrysalis, rein- forces their symbolism of rebirth and life after death. The spirit symbol is even more closely asssociated with moths than with butterflies, because moths usually fly at night. Carvings of moths appear on tombs in various parts of the world, representing spirits of the departed.

MOTHS AND BATS

Just as day-flying butterflies have to worry about attacks from hungry birds, night-flying moths must worry about the sharp teeth and open jaws of bats. Moths employ a number of defenses. Like butterflies, many moths are distasteful because their caterpillars have eaten toxic plants which discourage bats from attacking and swallowing them.

Bats find their moth prey in the dark by use of a very sophisticated echo-location system. The bat emits high-pitched sounds and listens for the echo that occurs when the sound is reflected off the moth. However, a moth is capable of hearing a bat's radar from a sufficient distance to enable the moth to take evasive action. In fact, the moth can hear the echo-location sounds well before the bat becomes aware of the presence of the moth.

If the moth hears an increased sound that indicates a bat is very close, it may fold its wings in the hopes of dropping quickly out of the bat's flight path.

Some moths are even capable of emitting their own ultrasonic signals which may warn a bat that has had previous unpleasant experiences that the potential prey does not taste good.

Tiger Moths

Family: Arctiidae

The brightly colored wings of some Tiger Moths have stripes like their namesake, the tiger. During the day, their bright colors advertise their poisonous nature to potential predators. A membrane on each side of the body produces an ultrasonic squeak to advertise their presence to bats which have also learned to avoid this distasteful moth.

Rattlebox Moth

The adult Rattlebox Moth, or Bella Moth, is active during the daytime and occurs in a multitude of color forms across much of Florida. It is one of the most variable tiger moths. Its conspicuous colors and its habit of flying during the day make this moth quite noticeable. It breeds continuously in Florida.

The Rattlebox Moth caterpillar makes a hole in the seed pod of the rattlebox plant and feeds on the highly toxic but nutritious seeds inside.

Utethesia bella. Range in Florida: Months seen: all year. Caterpillar food: legumes, elms, and Prunus species.

Giant Leopard Moth

The Giant Leopard Moth is also called the Eyed Tiger Moth. Its caterpillar is sometimes confused with the common Woolly Bear; however, the caterpillar of the Giant Leopard Moth is red or brown with stiff black hairs. This moth can be found at lights and is especially common at suburban or rural gas stations and motels with brightly lighted signs.

Ecpantheria scribonia, Wingspan: 2 to 3 1/2 inches. When seen: year round. Range: throughout Florida. Caterpillar food: wide variety of plants including cherry trees, cabbage and dandylions.

Acraea Moth

The Acrea Moth is also known as the Salt Marsh Moth. Its caterpillar is a well known agricultural pest.

Estigmene acrea. Wingspan: 2 1/2 inches. Range: throughout Florida. Months seen: especially common from October to May. Caterpillar food: many cultivated crops including corn, tobacco, cotton, watermelon, clover, cabbage, and peas.

△ An adult Acrea Moth, at rest, showing the tent-like, folded wings characteristic of the tiger moth family. This is the tiger moth most likely to be seen in Florida.
◁ The head of a tiger moth.

△ The same moth seen from the opposite side showing the yellow underside of both its wings and body. Most tiger moths have repellant glands behind their heads. Some of their larvae have irritating spines.

WOOLLY BEARS

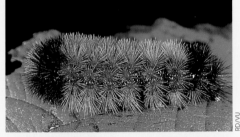

The caterpillars of the Isabella Tiger Moth are called "woolly bears," because of their furry appearance. They are famous, especially in Europe, because in folklore the amount of bright color in the middle of the body supposedly predicts the severity of winters. The more bright color, the shorter the winter. The woolly bears become less black and more reddish as they mature, so the differences in color actually show age differences in the caterpillars and are not a reliable indicator of the severity of the coming winter. The two photos above show how much the amount of reddish color can vary.

△ The yellow bubbles covering the head in this photo are a noxious, distasteful fluid oozing out from the front of the thorax as a defense when the moth is annoyed by a photographer or a potential predator.

Faithful Beauty Moth

The Faithful Beauty Moth is a colorful, day-flying member of the Tiger Moth family. Records from the turn of the century show that this moth was present at that time in the Florida Keys and South Florida. Recent studies show that its range has extended northward slightly. It is sometimes seen flying around the edges of hardwood hammocks.

Camposia fidelissima. Range in Florida: wherever oleanders are planted in South and Central Florida, it is more common from Miami through the Florida Keys. Caterpillar food: devil's potato, leafless cynanchum, and oleander.

Clear-winged Sphinx Moth

Family: Sphingidae

Hummingbird Clearwing Moth

The Hummingbird Clearwing benefits from its similarity to dangerous insects, such as wasps and bumblebees, because birds tend to avoid it as a source of food.

These moths have large transparent areas on the forewing and hindwing that lack scales. The caterpillar feeds on honeysuckle vines and hawthorns in Florida.

Hemaris thysbe. Maximum wingspread: 2 inches. Months seen: March to June and August to October. Generations per year: two. Caterpillar food: hawthorns, honeysuckle, and Prunus species.

△ A wing detail which shows the strikingly transparent areas.

△ Like the other sphinx moths, the Hummingbird Clearwing Moth feeds from deep-throated flowers while suspended in hovering flight. These moths are exclusively day-flying and mimic bumblebees for protection from predators.

△ The male Melonworm Moth emits sexual perfumes (pheromones) from the long scales on its tufted abdomen in order to attract the female to its display perch. These scent scales can be retracted when not in use.

Pyralid Moths

Family: Pyralidae

The Pyralids are the third largest moth family in North America with many small to medium-sized species whose larvae are important pests of agricultural crops, lawns, and ornamental plantings. Many species fly in the daytime and visit flowers. Several species also feed on beeswax as larvae! Some species have larvae that feed on stored grains and cereals. One group has larvae that are adapted to aquatic life and actually have gills to extract oxygen from pond water.

To pronounce this family name, be sure to place the accent on the second syllable: *Pie-ral'-id.*

Melonworm Moth

The Melonworm Moth is a common pest of crops such as cucumber, melons, squash, and pumpkins across the Gulf states. The pearly, translucent-white wings bordered by black are distinctive, along with the colorful tuft of anal scales.

Diaphania hyalinata. Maximimum wingspan: 1.1-1.2 inches. Months seen: all year except midwinter. Range in Florida: entire state.

Bagworm Moths

Family: Psychidae

These moths are famous for their caterpillars which carry their cocoons about with them while feeding The cocoons are decorated (camouflaged) with bits of vegetation such as leaves and twigs. The females never leave their cocoons, and the male moths fly only briefly before mating.

Bagworm Moth

After hatching, Bagworm Moth caterpillars build a case or bag using bits of plant material from their host plants. The caterpillars move about and feed without ever leaving the camouflaged protection of their bags.

The adult female is wingless and legless and never leaves her bag. When ready to mate, she releases a chemical which softens her bag so that her prospective mate can make an opening. Attracted by her sex pheromone, the male makes a small hole in the softened bag and mates with the female, that he never sees.

Afterwards, the female lays eggs inside the bag. She takes material from her body to plug the hole made by the male and dies shortly thereafter. When her eggs hatch, the caterpillars eat their way out and disperse to construct new bags.

Thyridopteryx ephemeraeformis. Range in Florida: entire state. Wingspan: 0.7 to 1.5 inches. Months seen: September through October. Caterpillar food: red cedar and other trees, shrubs, and herbaceous plants.

△ The Bagworm Moth larva carries its camouflaged case around with it as protection against predators. Bagworm Moth larvae each build their own individual case or bag using bits of plant material from their host plants. The larvae move about without ever leaving the camouflaged protection of their bags, and they pupate inside the bags.

▷ The Bagworm Moth forms its pupa inside this case.

BLOOD, SWEAT, AND TEARS

Butterflies and moths sip nectar through a tube which is normally rolled up under the "chin" and extended when needed to reach deep into flowers. However, some butterflies and moths sip the juice of rotting fruits as well as flower nectar, and in some parts of the world, certain moths have developed feeding tubes that are capable of puncturing fruit and extracting the juice. Other moths sip blood when it is available. One very remarkable moth, a rare species from Malaysia, has a feeding tube which is capable of penetrating flesh in a mosquito-like manner to extract blood. Still other moths are known to sip discharges from the eyes of large animals such as horses and buffalo. Tears and various other discharges from eyes are rich in nutrients. Captive moths have even sipped the tears of human researchers.

THE CLOTHES MOTH

The disgust some people feel for moths is no doubt related to the fact that one species of moth can consume clothing. The word moth comes from the old English "mothe," which means "gnawing vermin." The Clothes Moth is probably the moth mentioned in the Bible, as a symbol of corruption (Mathew 6:19). In days of old, Clothes Moths attacked books which were made a vellum, a lambskin used in bindings, but they are not a threat to modern bookbindings. Of course, it is the larva that does the destruction, especially of woolen clothing. Clothes Moths belong to the micromoth group, those less than one-half inch in length. They are not attracted to light like other moths; in fact, they can only survive a few hours in sunshine. Outdoors, Clothes Moth caterpillars prefer rotted wood or dried organic material, but inside a house, the caterpillars eat fur, wool and silk. They seem to be more attracted to soiled clothes. They are also a threat to many materials in museum collections. A variety of strong-smelling materials have been used through the centuries to repel them. Mothballs with camphor, popular a generation ago, were largely replaced with naphthalene, but now there are more effective repellants.

THE MEXICAN JUMPING BEAN IS A MOTH LARVA

The jumping bean moth lays eggs in pods of the arrow plant (yerba de flecha). The seeds inside the pod are consumed by the larvae of the moth. When uneaten seeds are ripe, they explode from the pods, but pods in which the seeds have been eaten just fall to the ground with the larva still inside. When the pod gets warm, when it is held in the hand, for instance, the larva inside grabs the silken walls with its legs and snaps its body, making the bean jump. The larva lives inside the pod for six months.

FLORIDA BUTTERFLY GARDENS

Florida offers the avid gardener a chance to attract butterflies every month of the year, especially in Central and South Florida. The best spot to plant a butterfly garden is an area that is sunny most of the day. This might be a small circle in the center of a tree-bordered lawn. Regardless of the circumstances, once attractive nectar sources and some larval foodplants are planted, butterflies will find them and make every day delightful by their frequent presence and fascinating behavior.

Nectar Plants

Not all flowers attract butterflies. For example, roses do not. However, most nurseries in Florida now maintain a special section for sun-loving plants which they label as "butterfly and hummingbird plants." These are generally plants with deep-throated flowers, sweet odors, bountiful nectar, and warm colors such as yellow, orange, or red. Select these plants carefully, planning for their growth to various heights. In the center of a circular garden, or at the back of a rectangular planting adjacent to a house wall, or fence, place the tallest plants, such as *Buddleia*, the butterfly bush.

Buddleia comes in various flower colors, including white, blue, deep purple, lavender, pink, and even yellow, depending on the species and cultivar. Most attractive to butterflies are the light blue, pink, and white bushes. *Buddleia* will bloom from summer through the fall in continuous floral abundance and will be covered with many kinds of butterflies throughout this period.

In front of the *Buddleia* (which could reach a height of 4 or 5 feet), plant the next tier of medium-sized perennials, such as

△ Butterfly bush (*Buddleia* sp.)

△ Multicolored impatiens

pentas (genus *Pentas*), and tropical milkweed (*Asclepias curassavica*). Pentas come in shades of white, red, pink, and purple, with most butterflies preferring the red pentas above all others. Tropical milkweed, sold in some Florida nurseries, is a tall, sparsely branched perennial with a cluster of yellow and orange flowers at the end of each stem. It blooms through the summer and fall.

Finally, in the front row of the butterfly garden, place low-growing plants such as impatiens, especially the salmon-orange, or red-flowered varieties. Impatiens prefer partial shade and plenty of water to be at their best. Other alternatives are purple alyssium, yellow sedum, and red and other brightly colored verbenas for the front row of your garden. All will attract many butterflies.

If there is plenty of space in the garden, try some large lantana bushes. Except for the prostrate varieties, lantana will grow to 4 or 5 feet in height if left untrimmed. Choose the purple variety or the mixed-color "roadside" variety to attract the widest range of butterflies. Yellow and orange-flowered lantana appeal to sulfurs and some skippers. The small, white lantana species, which is native to the Florida Keys, is also attractive to many butterflies.

In addition to the flowers mentioned in this section, try to observe what flowers seem to attract butterflies in a particular area. It would be hard to go wrong following these clues from nature.

Larval Foodplants

In addition to the adult nectar sources, don't neglect to plant caterpillar host plants. Read the butterfly species sections in this book to learn the caterpillar foods of the butterflies that you would like to attract and keep around your garden permanently

(provided you live within their range). Then seek out these foodplants at a local nursery. Native plant nurseries are especially good sources of the plants that caterpillars like but which may not have particularly bright flowers.

Plant passionflower vines, especially the native purple passionflower, on a fence or wall. Besides producing spectacular blooms, these vines will prove irresistible to the Gulf Fritillaries, Zebras, and Julias. In the southern part of Florida, butterflies are attracted year-round to passionflower vines if they are kept well-watered and fertilized. In central and north Florida, passionflower vines will attract long-winged butterflies at least six months of the year.

Also plant some pipevines (*Aristolochia*), to attract the Pipevine Swallowtail

△ Cabbage White butterfly on blazing star.

and the Polydamus Swallowtail. These butterflies start flying in March and can be found throughout the state by mid-summer. The adults avidly visit lantana plants for nectar, while their caterpillars happily chomp on the pipevines. Try parsley or other members of the carrot family, such as dill, to attract the Black Swallowtail.

Paw-paw trees attract Zebra Swallowtails. Spicebush plants attract Spicebush

tails. Spicebush plants attract Spicebush Swallowtails. Milkweed plants (*Aslcepias*) attract Monarchs and Queens anywhere in Florida. The females will lay eggs on these plants after sipping the nectar.

People living along either coast in northern Florida may plant a couple of southern red cedars and perhaps will be lucky enough to get a Sweadner's Hairstreak colony established on these trees. Try shredding some mistletoe berries (of broad-leafed mistletoe species) on the upper side of the branches of a sycamore or sweet gum, and rubbing the exposed mistletoe seeds into the cracks of the tree bark. This will establish some of the broad-leaf mistletoe plants onto the tree and provide a larval food-plant for the Great Blue Hairstreak.

Plant some vegetables such as cabbages, radishes, mustards, and other crucifers to attract the Cabbage White and its relatives. Some alfalfa seed scattered in an abandoned field or corner of a lot will allow the Alfalfa Sulfur to get established, at least in north Florida. If space is available, plant some *Cassia* trees or bushes along the prop-

△ Roadside lantana

erty line as a background for a butterfly garden. Cassia will attract large female sulphurs, such as the Cloudless Sulphur, to lay their eggs .

An ordinary lawn, of St. Augustine grass, can provide food for several species of skippers as well as satyrid butterflies. A hackberry tree may attract the Hackberry Butterfly or the Tawny Emperor. Willows planted in a wet spot may bring in Viceroys plus many species of moths. Wild cherry (*Prunus serotina* and *P. virginiana*) may be available from a nursery. This tree will attract Red-spotted Purple butterflies.

As butterflies start to fill a garden, it will be tempting to try to attract an ever-increasing variety of species. Local botanical gardens may be willing to help by selling

△ Thistle going to seed

some of their excess stock. The major butterfly display houses in Florida, including Butterfly World at Coconut Creek, by the Florida Turnpike, and Wings of Wonder at Cypress Gardens, have hundreds of plants for sale in their nurseries, and also books on butterfly gardening for both beginners and

△ Native milkweed.

BUTTERFLY CONSERVATION

To most Floridians, butterflies seem to be everywhere. Abundant and flying in every month of the year, they make life more stimulating and interesting by their colorful presence. Yet when Florida's butterfly fauna is compared with that of other states, the result is not impressive. Florida has about 160 resident species of butterflies that actually breed in the state. Compared to Colorado's 250 species, California's 269 species, over 300 species in Texas, and at least 320 species in Arizona, Florida's subtropical paradise is seemingly not as hospitable as we might like to think.

It is hard to know how many species of butterflies once lived in Florida before humans came and began transforming the landscape. But one thing we do know is that much of the natural landscape of Florida has disappeared under the hand of man. In North Florida, timber reserves for pulpwood industries, all planted by man, replace the original vegetation. In Central Florida, thousands of acres of natural habitat were

transformed early in this century into citrus groves and other farmland. In recent years, massive developments for housing and recreation industries have dominated the landscape. In southern Florida, huge areas have been converted to urban housing. Sugar cane fields, orchards, turf farms, and vegetable croplands have replaced natural vegetation. To a butterfly, tree farms and citrus groves are ecological "deserts," lacking larval foodplants and adult nectar sources.

Massive spraying for mosquito control and agricultural pest control, together with herbicide spraying along roadsides, has also contributed to the loss of butterflies.

There is only one species of butterfly in the state that is formally classified as an endangered species by the federal government and the State of Florida—that is the Schaus Swallowtail butterfly, found only in the northern Keys today. But there are many butterfly species, at least 60 in fact, whose populations have been greatly reduced in Florida, and will soon join the Schaus Swallowtail if their habitat is not preserved.

We can help in a small but effective way by supporting conservation of wild habitat areas for all organisms, including butterflies. We can join the nationwide "Bring Back the Butterflies" campaign started by Ronald Boender, owner of Butterfly World in south Florida. Butterfly World has been effectively promoting the idea of butterfly gardening as a means of conservation. It is surprising how quickly cultivating the proper plants can attract butterflies. Within a few weeks, a home or local park can be enlivened with hundreds of butterflies that weren't there before. Able to survive and reproduce because of human efforts, these butterflies in turn will provide a nucleus for re-establishing themselves in other parts of the region, as long as suitable habitat remains.

Free literature is available from Butterfly World, and many books have been written specifically about butterfly gardening. Our small efforts can have a large impact when it comes to preserving Florida's butterflies, some of the most beautiful creatures on earth.

△ This photo shows research scientists in French Guiana studying and photographing moths attracted to a white cloth by a mercury vapor lamp. On a good, moonless night in a tropical country, the number and variety of moths that can be attracted with this type of equipment is truly awesome. As can be seen from this photograph, the vast majority of moths belong to a group called micromoths, those less than one half inch in size.

ATTRACTING MOTHS WITH BLACKLIGHT

It is possible to see many of the beautiful moths that fly through the dark of night. Just purchase a blacklight or a mercury vapor lamp (better, but more expensive) and position it to shine onto a white sheet. Most Florida backyards will yield many interesting moths. Of course, remote wooded locations might be better. This is the method used by research scientists working in rainforests. It is fairly inexpensive and a source of endless interest for families wishing to view the amazing creatures that frequent their yards at night, but are seldom seen. Blacklights are available from BioQuip (Gardena, California). They operate on 110 volts AC or a 12 volt battery, including a car cigarette lighter adaptor.

Another technique for attracting moths is to smear onto a tree trunk a paste made from a mixture of sweets such as sugar or molasses, plus a fermented brew such as beer or rum. Moths are attracted to tree sap and this is a simple substitute. The moths that appear can be observed with a flashlight at intervals through the night.

WATCHING VERSUS COLLECTING

Traditionally, those with an interest in butterflies took great pride in building large collections of mounted specimens. However, a growing number of enthusiasts who find no pleasure in dispatching their winged friends in a killing jar, satisfy their interest by observing, photographing, and recording the behavior of butterflies. Those with a competitive streak work to expand lists of species they have observed in the wild, much like bird listers.

There is a tendency to label everything and everybody. Butterfly enthusiasts have been promoting the name "butterflyers," to describe the group of people devoted to this hobby. This follows closely the trend of replacing the name "bird-watcher" with "birder." In fact, birders and butterfliers are often the same people, so it is not surprising that recently they have been organizing themselves along the same lines.

Just as birders have their annual National Audubon Society's Christmas Bird Count, butterflyers now have a Fourth of July Butterfly Count which serves the same function. Volunteers spend the day observing and recording the numbers of each species they have observed. These data are compiled by the North American Butterfly Association to help present a nationwide picture of butterfly populations.

All this is not to say that collecting no longer has a legitimate scientific purpose. In fact, butterfly collections have proved invaluable to researchers for documenting the kinds of species in each area, their ranges, their variation in color and pattern, and for conservation purposes such as charting the decline of populations in certain areas.

BUTTERFLY WATCHING ACTIVITIES

For those who prefer to observe rather than collect butterflies, the sheer joy of watching these beautiful creatures may be enough to maintain a lifetime of interest. However, enjoyment can be enhanced with increased knowledge of butterflies. The beginner can start with just his naked eyes and this book in hand. Here are some things to observe which can add to the enjoyment.

Interactions: Butterflies are never alone, whether in the woods or in the garden. They are part of a complex ecosystem and the observer will frequently see them interacting with predators, with parasites, with other butterflies, and even with the human observer. Much can be learned from these encounters. For example, after watching a bird chase a butterfly, if the butterfly escapes unharmed, give some thought to how it managed to survive. Was the butterfly more agile than the bird? Did it seek shelter in a place the bird could not follow? Was the bird fooled by a tail or an eyespot into attacking the butterfly's wing instead of its head or body?

Courtship versus Territory: When two butterflies are following each other, fluttering about together, are they courting or battling for territory? If it is a male and female, then the answer is simple, since territorial disputes only occur between males. But it may be hard to determine the sex of a butterfly in rapid flight. This is especially true for a beginner who is not totally familiar with the differences in the markings which would reveal this information to a more experienced observer. Here are things to look for that might explain what is happening in a butterfly chase scene: Does one individual try to hover over another in flight, rather than trying to hit it or fly furiously at it? If so, it is probably a male, wafting its pheromone scent over a female to seduce it. Does one individual attempt to force the other to land on the ground or a nearby leaf, rather than chase it away in a straight line or in upward flight? If so, it is probably a male trying to get the female to alight so that the male can land next to her and attempt copulation.

Listing: Like birdwatchers, many butterfly watchers keep a record of the different species they have seen and identified in their own garden. It might also be fun to keep a list of all the species personally observed in the wild anywhere in the world. Birders call this their "life list" and take great pride in expanding it. To prove that a butterfly listed was actually the species observed, it is useful to write a description of the butterfly as it appeared and later compare all the details with a photograph from this book or a scientific description from a field guide. Some of the points to observe include size, color and pattern of the upperside and underside of the wings, and the flight pattern (fast or slow; erratic or straight). What kind of flowers did it visit? What kind of plants did it lay eggs on if it was a female? What type of habitat was it in?

Marking Butterflies: The butterflies in a garden can be studied more carefully by marking a few specimens. Using a homemade insect net, or one purchased from a biological supply, carefutly trap a butterfly. Hold it gently but firmly by the thorax and use a permanent marker to put a number on the underside of its wings. Marking, if done carefully, will not harm the butterfly. After the butterfly is released, its activities will be easy to study without recapturing it.

Much valuable information can be gathered by a patient observer. Does the butterfly return to the same feeding area every day? Does it go to a particular roosting spot at night? Does it fly in a particular direction when it arrives at the garden and another when it leaves? Are these directions the same every day? Does it visit the same flowers in the same sequence? This might indicate that it has memorized a feeding route. Does it arrive at the same time every day? This might indicate that there are special times when the nectar in the flowers is at its fullest.

Seasonal Color Variations: Most species of butterflies go through several generations each year. Often the color of each generation is a bit different (especially for the following Florida species: Barred Sulphur, Sleepy Orange, Dainty Sulphur, and Zebra Swallowtail). For example, the colors may become darker in the fall. The careful observer can see these changes over the course of a year and compare one year with another to establish a pattern.

More Sophisticated Studies—Ranges and Vagrants: Among the most popular activities with birdwatchers (after listing) is studying the range of birds, that is, the limits of the area where they are usually found. This same activity is also scientifically useful with butterflies. Learn the generally accepted range of a certain species and then look for changes in this range. Is this species expanding the area in which it is usually found, or is the area contracting? Sightings beyond the normal range which are well documented become valuable information for researchers.

There is also the possibility of sighting "vagrants," butterflies which are far out of their normal range for a variety of reasons.

They may have been blown off course during migration by powerful storms, they may have been trapped inside a truck and inadvertantly been transported to another region before escaping, they may have travelled to their new location as eggs, larvae, or pupae on nursery plants, or they may have simply lost their way. In any case, the presence of vagrants does not indicate that the range of a butterfly species has changed. Observing a species which does not belong where it has been sighted can be exciting. However, knowing when one is observing something unusual is the result of experience and much study.

More Sophisticated Tools—Camera and Camcorder: Butterfly photography is an excellent way to observe butterflies close-up without harming them. All that is required to get started is a close-up lens, preferably one with a slightly long focal length (such as 105 mm) which makes it possible to photograph from a reasonable distance of a few feet. A normal lens can be used with extension tubes as a less expensive alternative, but requires a very close approach. Many opportunities will be missed when the butterfly has been frightened away.

A camcorder is easier to use than a camera and most models include a zoom lens which will allow recording from a reasonable distance. The camcorder also allows the recording of behavior which can be studied later at a leisurely pace and discussed with others who are more expert.

Something New: As the butterfly watcher becomes more sophisticated, there is always the chance that he will observe something that has never been seen or noticed before. This is how the pollen-feeding behavior of Heliconius butterflies was discovered (see page 25 for details about this behavior). Dr. Larry Gilbert of the University of Texas raised Heliconius butterflies in his own Texas greenhouse. While watching them one day as he was watering his plants, he noticed the butterflies gathering pollen and deliberately putting it on the outside of their proboscises.

BUTTERFLY ORGANIZATIONS

North American Butterfly Association
4 Delaware Road
Morristown New Jersey 07960
(Publishes a beautiful color journal quarterly that is especially suitable for butterfly watchers and gardeners)

Association for Tropical Lepidoptera
1717 NW 45th Avenue
Gainesville, FL 32605
(Publishes two colorful journals which are suitable for either amateurs or professionals)

The Lepidoptera Research Foundation
c/o Santa Barbara Museum of
Natural History
2559 Puesta del Sol Road
Santa Barbara, CA 93105
(Publishes a colorful journal for professionals)

The Lepidopterists' Society
c/o Natural History Museum
900 Exposition Boulevard
Los Angeles, CA 90007
(Publications of interest to the amateur and the professional)

The Monarch Program
P.O. Box 178671
San Diego, CA 92177
(Publishes an interesting monthly newsletter about Monarchs and other butterflies)

Southern Lepidopterists' Society
5421 NW 69th Lane
Gainesville, FL 32653
(Publishes frequent newletters)

The Xerces Society
10 Southwest Ash Street
Portland, OR 97204
(Publishes a quarterly magazine about conservation topics. The Xerces Society was named after the Xerces Blue butterfly which used to inhabit sand dunes near San Francisco and became the first American butterfly known to become extinct because of human activities. The Xerces Society is concerned with all invertebrates, not just butterflies.)

Young Entomologist's Society
c/o Department of Entomology
Michigan State University
East Lansing, MI 48824
(Publishes a quarterly journal suitable for students through high school.)

TABLE OF CONTENTS